MW01037515

THE DIALOGUE
—————— *of* ——————
EARTH AND SKY

THE DIALOGUE
of
EARTH AND SKY

Dreams, Souls, Curing,
and the Modern Aztec Underworld

TIMOTHY J. KNAB

THE UNIVERSITY OF ARIZONA PRESS
TUCSON

The University of Arizona Press
Text © 2004 Timothy J. Knab
Illustrations © 2004 Benjamín Fierro
All rights reserved

First paperback printing 2009
ISBN 978-0-8165-2880-6 (pbk. : alk. paper)

Library of Congress Cataloging-in-Publication Data
Knab, T. J.
    The dialogue of earth and sky : dreams, souls, curing, and the
modern Aztec underworld / Timothy J. Knab.
        p. cm.
    Includes bibliographical references and index.
    ISBN 0-8165-2413-0 (cloth : alk. paper)
    1. Aztecs—Religion. 2. Indians of Mexico—Religion.
3. Sierra Norte (Oaxaca, Mexico)—Social life and customs. I. Title.
    F1219.76.R45K58   2004
    299.7—dc22
    2004006911

Manufactured in the United States of America on acid-free, archival-
quality paper and processed chlorine free.

14   13   12   11   7   6   5   4   3

For My Tlamatini,

For Doris Heyden

CONTENTS

ILLUSTRATIONS

Acknowledgments

The tradition that I inherited from Doña Rubia and Don Inocente in the Sierra Norte de Puebla is but a reconstructed memory, though I practice it to this day. I write ethnography as fiction (Knab 1995) and analysis as fact; one evokes a reality and the other seeks to understand it. This is my understanding of the dialogue of earth and sky that continues to this day in the Sierra de Puebla. In this sense, the real facts of ethnography are in the interpretations and representations of the "other" and should thus remain fictions. The tools of fiction are so much better suited to representation that I prefer them as a means of writing good ethnography.

The drafts of this book were written long before *A War of Witches* (Knab 1995), and in fact, it was an early version of this manuscript that, when it was seized by Chinese authorities on our way into Tibet, led to my formulation of *Witches*. Peter Shotwell, Edwina Williams, Larry Sullivan, and my audience of trekkers, tourists, travelers, and pilgrims helped me to see that through ethnographically accurate fiction I could tell a tale that was both true and interesting. Good ethnography requires years of commitment, and good ethnographic fiction, though more rewarding, is far more difficult to write than a simple monograph. An early draft of this manuscript was essential before writing *A War of Witches*.

Without the help, commitment, encouragement, and knowledge of the residents of San Martín, I would never have reached the understanding I have today of their world. Learning the language, traditions, and ways of Sanmartinos was in no way as important as the deep and long-lasting friendships I forged with the many villagers who helped me to understand everyday life in San Martín. Some names and locations have been changed for the sake of present-day villagers.

My teachers, colleagues, and friends in both the United States and Mexico, Peter T. Furst and Jill Leslie McKeever Furst, Gary Gossen, Dennis and Barbara Tedlock, Jorge Klor de Alva, Duncan Earle, Richard Haily, Davíd Carrasco, Tony Aveni, Nigel Davies, John Carlson, Barbara J. Price, Bill Fowler, Johanna Broda, Linda Manzanilla, Evelyn Rattray, Shelton P. Applegate III, Bill Sanders, Alfredo López Austin, Luis Vargas, Mercedes Olivera, Pat Plunket, Gabriela Uruñuela, Ignacio Bernal, Eckhart Boege,

Jacques Galinier, B. J. Isbell, Jaimie Litvak King, Naomi Quezada, Dave Grove, Beatrice Braniff, Donald and Dorothy Cordry all influenced this work at different points. Paul Rich's gardens at the Universidad de las Américas, Puebla, gave me a place to contemplate this work. I owe particular thanks to Prof. Paul Kirchhoff, who did not think that this material could exist; Fernando Horcacitas, who was sure that somewhere such things must exist; and Thelma D. Sullivan, who constantly encouraged this work.

Doris Heyden, one of the great nurturing mothers of Mexican anthropology, provided counsel and criticism throughout my work on this material. She also provided a welcome invitation not only to me, but to anyone else vitally interested in Mesoamerican anthropology. Now that she has been stricken silent, it is for her that I am writing this book.

The editing, revising, and rethinking of this book was immensely aided by Peter Shotwell, Jaye Shore Freyer, Josefina Morales, Alan Sandstrom, María Elena Gómez Huerta, Tomás Sanchez Sanchez, Jill Leslie McKeever Furst, Peter T. Furst, Miguel Jimenez Díaz, Duncan Earle, Pedro Lujan, Jeanne Simonelli, Dennis and Barbara Tedlock, as well as several anonymous readers. Benjamín Fierro's illustrations have contributed a refinement to this book that I never could have achieved. The work upon which this book is based was supported by grants from the National Endowment for the Humanities, the American Philosophical Society, the Instituto de Investigaciones Antropológicas of the Universidad Nacional Autónoma de México, and the Universidad de las Américas, Puebla. My alma mater, the Universidad de las Américas, Puebla, has made this book possible. The formulations here are my own, but they rely on the work of many, many others in the field of Mesoamerican anthropology who are not cited here or in the text. My students at the Universidad de las Américas, Puebla also merit my sincere gratitude for their insightful commentaries. Finally, the contribution of the editors working with the University of Arizona Press, Christine Szuter, Allyson Carter, Harrison Shaffer, and Simone Solondz, has been invaluable. The time, thoroughness, and care they have dedicated to preparing this volume has made it a far better book.

This book is based on the tradition of one woman, Doña Rufina Raimirez Manzano, and her compadre Don Inocencio Flores. For many years I was under the impression that I was the last in a long line of curers to learn this tradition. I was also under the impression that this was the kind of private and personal tradition that would make this book ethically impossible to write and publish. However in 1991, when I realized that there were many other followers of the tradition, I also realized that Doña Rufina had taught me her way of exploring the underworld of her ancestors for a reason. She wanted it known. There is in fact nothing so secret or private about being of service to the Most Holy Earth that it is not common knowledge among specialists, including the techniques of witchcraft, which are, in the end, methods for murder. By teaching me her tradition, Doña Rufina hoped to achieve two goals: showing the compassion, caring, and consideration required of practitioners serving the Most Holy Earth; and exposing the sinister aspects of the tradition in order to thwart those who would stray from what she knew was the "good path." This book and *A War of Witches* are the reasons Rufina chose to share her tradition.

The "Path"

IT IS NOW NEARLY THIRTY YEARS since I began to discover the profound beliefs that the people of the Sierra de Puebla still maintain in the Most Holy Earth. Early in my work, many people told me that such beliefs had long since disappeared into the nebulous past, but in San Martín I found that they had not. These beliefs were still a part of everyday life almost five hundred years after the Spanish conquest. It was not until 1991 that I learned how this system had survived the onslaught of Catholicism, colonialism, and the modern world.

It had been almost ten years since I last visited San Martín when I went there in 1991 after a conference on Pilgrimage and Processions in Cholula at the Universidad de las Américas, Puebla. In my long absence, both Doña Rubia and Don Inocente had died, and I didn't know whether there were any people who would still remember me. There were, however, and I spent a pleasant day visiting and gossiping with old friends.

I had been initiated as a dreamer, and I thought I knew a great deal about the people of San Martín and the tradition that Doña Rubia and Don Inocente had passed on to me. The prayers and techniques for curing the human soul that I had learned were, I thought, unique. However, I was due for one more surprise.

It was long past dark by the time I was able to break away from the gossip and began the trip back to Cuetzalan from San Martín. As I trudged along the stony road in the moonless night, I looked up at the graveyard on the hill above town where Rubia was buried, realizing that I couldn't climb the hill in the middle of the night. That would lay me open to suspicion of witchcraft. On the other hand, the locals believed that murdered people's souls would do anything for a few extra days of life, so no one went near the cemetery at night and no one would be around to see me.

Thinking these thoughts, I was looking up the hill and suddenly noticed flickering candlelight through the overgrown brush in the center of the graveyard where the chapel was. As I drew closer, I could hear something that sounded like prayers, but I couldn't tell in what language they were being said. The road circled the hill for a little while, and I followed it in the darkness, trying to listen to what was going on, until I came to where the path to Cuetzalan separated from the road.

At this point, there was a stone wall and a house, and from the dark recesses of the yard, I could hear someone call for me to come in. It was Don Ignacio, a fat, jolly man whom I had known for many years and had seen this morning in the market. The urgency in his voice told me that this would not be a social visit. With what was going on up on the hill, I quickly opened his gate, despite the barking of his dogs.

As I came into the yard of the house, he greeted me, in Nahuat, "It is darkening. Are you on the way to see your friends of the night up there?"

"Which ones?" I asked. Since Don Inocente had died, I knew no one I would call a 'friend of the night' in San Martín. The term usually referred to a witch, or *curandero,* someone well trained in the old ways. "You know which things they are," Don Ignacio said cryptically. He was not even using the personal particle in Nahuat, but rather the one for objects.

"What are they?" I asked.

"You know them!" he said.

"They are friends of yours, alright," he said, as if he didn't hear me. "They were friends of those two old witches, Inocente and Rubia, so they must be friends of yours: brothers and sisters, women who do not have men, fathers with no children. They follow the same way. Aren't you going up there for them?" he asked.

"Well, maybe," I replied cagily, put off by Don Ignacio's respectful tone in speaking about these "things" who were clearly people I was expected to know. I knew he had especially feared old Inocente.

"Can't you hear them?" he asked, handing me a flashlight. "They've been waiting for you."

Slowly, I picked my way up the overgrown path to the graveyard. I had been told that Doña Rubia's grave was off to the southern side, where it was peaceful. Finally, I stood before the dark wooden open doors of the chapel in the graveyard of San Martín. I could see five or six people through the haze of the burning copal incense, but no one I could recognize. I could hear their voices, though, and there was one voice that was praying in the same way I had been taught to pray by Doña Rubia.

They were grouped around a man in the center who was using the highland dialect of Modern Aztec. My Nahuat was quite rusty, but I could still understand most of the prayer. It was one of those that beseeches the Holy Earth to take back the souls of the dead that had escaped. It was a prayer to lure them back and make them comfortable.

These people had obviously seen me enter the chapel, and one of the figures from the penumbra began moving toward me. Since they were supposed to be friends of my mentor, Doña Rubia, I decided to greet the man in the darkness with an archaic phrase that she had taught me: "*Tlalocan*, the good night, may it cover you with fine words and hear you."

The dark figure repeated my greeting and put out his hand to touch my shoulder. This is the way one greets close friends or ritual kinsmen in the village. I responded by touching his shoulder, and he motioned me toward the back of the chapel. As I got closer, I saw a semicircle of candles with two incense burners at the ends on the long table that passed for an altar. There was a large single candle in the center. Lying outside the curve of flickering lights were offerings: a bowl of water, flowers, tortillas, a plate of beans, cigarettes, and a bottle of *aguardiente*.

One by one, each of the members of the group who had been standing around the altar, five men and one woman, came forward. I recognized none of these people, yet we all greeted each other as ritual brothers and sisters.

Finally, one of the men spoke to me.

"Don Timoteo," (he knew my name, though I had never seen him before in my life) "are you not the brother of Doña Rubia who lies here in the Most Holy Earth?" The term for brother is an archaic and honorific form most unusual in Modern Aztec speech.

I replied that I was the son, or heir, of Doña Rubia who did lie here in the Most Holy Earth.

"This we know," the man said, "and she is well. We see her in dreams where her soul wanders about in the house of women. She is among the midwives and honored women there. She is safe in her home there. But here in San Martín there has been much sickness, and it comes from these dead who do not know how to find their homes in the earth, those who have not been embraced by our mother, our father, the true *taloc*. They are disturbing the living."

This was a group of practitioners who followed the 'good path.' I had long ago heard both Rubia and Inocente refer to their traditional practices and prayers in this way. Though I knew that there were others who shared the same practices, I had never known any of them. I nevertheless was asked to join them in the task of returning souls to the underworld.

Afterwards, one of the men told me, "Well, you know there's this man in Puebla who can remember his 'ancestors' back to the time of Don Juan Manuel Antonio Mixcua, Don Juan Manuel Martin Ocelo, Don Manuel Antonio Francisco Hernandez, Don Martín Antonio Francisco Abad, José Antonio Martín Luz, Juan Francisco Martín Luz, and all of our fathers of the light."

Were these the names, I asked myself, of the martyred leaders of messianic Nahua movements in the sixteenth and seventeenth centuries? Some of them certainly were. They were always invoked in prayers. They, as well as others, such as San Juan Lucero de la Mañana and San Juan Crencia de Dios, both aspects of Venus, stood like sentries at the edges of the world separating earth from sky. They kept the traditions of the ancestors separate from those of the sky. They were the teachers of the 'good path' and the ancestors of the followers of the 'good path,' its defenders and patrons.

"They're our real ancestors," he said. "They were the ones who found the 'good path' and taught us to know our *naguals*. They had all these things written in books, but then the books were stolen and burned by the Spaniards, by the Mexicans. They were the people who could see clearly in the darkness of *talocan*.

"They brought what they remembered into the caves, those priests of *talocan*. They hid in the caves, in the darkness. They showed our people how to pray and make offerings so they could recite all the prayers of the ancestors and they could read the luck of the days," he continued. "They became our special patrons, our assistants in searching out lost souls in *talocan,* the world of the ancestors we visit in our dreams. When the dreams don't want to come from the earth, they help us."

These were all people who followed the same tradition that I had been taught by Doña Rubia. There were people in this group who prayed in Spanish, Náhuatl, Otomí, and Tótonac, and they told me of many others who followed the same tradition.

I thought I was the last individual to learn this tradition from Doña Rubia. She taught no one else from San Martín the tradition before her death in 1986. Now she was buried but a few feet from where I was standing. The sky began to redden slightly through the cloudy mists. I could almost hear her mischievous chuckle, as I learned what she had never told me, that there were others, many others, who followed the same *cualli ohti,* the 'good path.' And now they were talking without fear.

I returned to Puebla with one of the men I had met in the chapel and was introduced to several other practitioners. Slowly and meticulously, I got names and addresses of others who shared the same tradition in Mexico City, Guerrero, and Aguascalientes. When I returned to Mexico City, I found even more followers of this same tradition, and though I didn't have long to talk with them, I could see that there was a homogeneity in their practice. The prayers and the techniques of dreaming to cure the soul were essentially the same as those I had learned.

Though many of them did not see dreams as journeys to the underworld, they all used dreams as a projective mechanism in curing to restore imbalances perceived in the human soul. This was a practical method of treatment that had been used for perhaps centuries. Was this, I wondered, how traditions such as those cited by Ruíz de Alarcón (1987[1629]) were preserved? Did practitioners function like a secret society, training only a handful of followers? Were there other organizations such as this one? I had heard of a fraternal group in Veracruz called the *Señores de Noche,* which even supported a clinic, and of other groups as well in Oaxaca and Morelos, but were these all similar groups of curers training apprentices in a tradition? I did not have time to find out in 1991 if this was the case.

When I returned to Mexico in 1992, I found several other practitioners of the tradition I had learned and also found that the knowledge of *talocan* and the underworld that I had thought was localized to the Sierra de Puebla was in fact not unique. Practitioners and laymen alike in villages that had been well studied for many years when interviewed in Nahuatl could, and did, easily discuss *tlalocan* and the nature of the lords of the earth. Why, I asked some of the men from one village who had worked for eminent archaeologists, had they never mentioned this? "No one asked," was the reply.

It is perhaps as Sandstrom (1991: 231–32) has noted, that this is knowledge that is taken for granted, and unless one asks in the proper way, in the proper language, it will remain part of the assumed reality differentiating us from them, native from outsider.

This tradition is Doña Rubia's own synthesis of the essential factors of tradition and ethos that make her practice meaningful and understandable. This is a Mesoamerican system and synthesis of the natural and the supernatural worlds that has been typical of the region for centuries, perhaps millennia. It is unique, yet it follows a path as old as the earth itself in Mesoamerica.

When I began the process of learning the way of the Most Holy Earth (Knab 1995), what I agreed to do was, I had thought, impossible. Perhaps it was not. A friend of mine from graduate school, Barbara Tedlock, had followed this path with her husband Dennis, both becoming Quiche diviners (B. Tedlock 1982), as had my former graduate school roommate Duncan Earle. It required a suspension of disbelief and a commitment of service to the world of the ancestors and its children, present-day Sanmartinos. Most of the material in this book is based on that process and what the two old curers taught me about following the 'good path' and curing the maladies of the human soul.

What Doña Rubia and Don Inocente taught me and what I took it upon myself to learn were not necessarily the same things. I had to learn far more than simply how to perform a narrative or say a prayer. I had to learn to cure the human soul. I had to learn a whole system vastly different from anything within my experience, and I had to learn to serve those whose system it was.

I could not be satisfied with learning simply the structure, or form, the outward manifestation of the system. I had to learn to use it to help those I served. What I learned was to apply with knowledge and compassion the heuristic methods and understandings that I had reached of their system. I learned that this was what Rubia and Inocente did, and it was what they expected me to do.

Simply comprehending a world so far removed from my own required that I put it in a perspective that was its own and that I let the principles of the phenomena dictate their own form (Schutz 1967). The fictions and shorthands that I developed in the process of understanding how to use this system are my own, a theory of practice far removed from that of Pierre Bourdieu (1977), more a theory of practical knowledge.

This is the result of a dialogue that I have carried on over the years with both the material and its representation (D. Tedlock 1983; D. Tedlock and Mannheim 1995). Little did I realize when I began this process that Voloshinov's *Marxism and the Philosophy of Language* (1973), a work I had cut my teeth on in linguistics at the Escuela Nacional de Antropología e Historia, was actually the work of M. M. Bakhtin (Clark and Holquist 1984), the father of dialogic thinking. The dialogic process has turned out to be crucial for my understanding of the traditions of San Martin, for it is only through dialogue that this system emerges.

The voices of the individuals whose tradition this is have passed to the world of the ancestors, yet they can be heard throughout the exposition. The prayers and dreamtales are taken from tapes and field notes.

Exposition is perhaps not the best way to recount this tradition—just as dreamtales are most clearly understood through constant dialogue rather than by recounting one's understanding of a client and a dream—yet it is perhaps the clearest way to present a complex tradition. It is based on a constant dialogue of practical knowledge of a specific tradition.

The form of the exposition is not one that either Rubia or Inocente would necessarily approve. Their knowledge was practical and learned through experience, not exposition. Initially both of them were consultants and readers for each paper I wrote on their tradition. Without them, it is my responsibility to formulate the material in a coherent way. Several other traditional healers read parts of this book in Spanish, and one read the entire manuscript in English and made extensive comments. The exposition, which is the body of this book, provides a framework for a multiplicity of interpretations from a multiplicity of disciplines. This is an interpretation of a tradition that is perhaps unique, for any representation is in fact an interpretation (Todorov 1982b), but this one results from the practical experience of learning to apply basic principles of a Meso-american cosmovision.

The material discussed here is the province of specialists; it is not general knowledge in the culture. Of course, bits and pieces of it are part of the general knowledge, but its interpretation and integration into a coherent whole is the province of specialists.

Much of this material is based on an astute observation of the natural world (McKeever Furst 1995); much is based on traditions, metaphors, and meanings (Knab 1984); and much is based on the interpretation that I have given it in the context of Mesoamerica. This is what Radin (1955) and Miguel León-Portilla (1963) have looked at as a branch of philosophy. Other researchers with other interests and from other disciplines would perhaps interpret it in other ways—as a traditional psychology of the spirit, traditional medicine, a group sociology, a natural philosophy, geography of the unknown, or religion. That is their post-modern prerogative.

Necessarily, this book begins with the role of the human soul in life on the earth, an ecology of the spirit, for it is on the basis of this practical knowledge that most of the notions about dreams and the underworld are founded. Maintaining life on the earth, maintaining the balance of body and soul in the world, is the dialogue of earth and sky. The first chapter on notions of the soul is essential for understanding curing practices and the role dreams play in that process.

The second chapter concerns the role of dreams in everyday life in the village. There are dreams that cure, but these are not the only dreams that are important. Dreams, no matter what their nature, are important to Sanmartinos. A general discussion of dreams, as they are viewed by both specialists and non-specialists, is essential before venturing into the world of the ancestors. There are standard narrative genres that are employed for recounting dreams and tales of the underworld in San Martín, as there are set techniques for talking about dreamtime experiences. Native practitioners employ a highly sophisticated technique, drawing on their specialized knowledge of the traditions of the ancestors and the underworld to recount dreams. Dreams are a vital part of everyday life in the village, yet only a few initiates can travel in their dreams to the underworld of their ancestors at will in search of a lost soul. This is the duty of specially trained practitioners.

The third chapter consists of the prayers that are the templates for comparing the world of the ancestors with the waking world. They are a primary part of the rituals for dreaming and curing maladies of the human soul. The prayers are at first learned by rote. Then as the practitioner becomes more knowledgeable and adept, they are modified and expanded. Prayer is an art for communicant and the ancestors. It beseeches, cajoles, threatens, entreats, and also instructs. The relationships maintained by humankind with the realms of the supernatural are concretized in prayer.

Learning the form and structure of the underworld is an essential part of every practitioner's training. Learning to recount dreams, forming a dreamtale, 'carrying it on one's back' to the waking world, is but the first part of the practitioner's labor in curing.

The fourth chapter is an exploration of the form and geography of the underworld of the ancestors, the world of dreams. The curer must learn the form and geography of this world to successfully recount the journeys of the soul in dreamtime. Dreamtales are far more than parables in this world; they embody the ethos and cosmovision that link Sanmartinos with their traditions and the Most Holy Earth, *talocan*.

The fifth chapter focuses on the dialogics of curing and the meta-language of dreams as a tool in curing the afflicted soul. This metalanguage brings tradition together with the events of everyday life in a technique that allows clients and their families to carry on a dialogue concerning their own problems in the world. The dialogic interpretation of dreams is the practitioner's primary instrument, combined with practical and rational ritual, for restoring a client's soul to its proper equilibrium and thus curing him or her. The exposition of this system of curing and dreaming shows that it is a practical method of finding and resolving the problems of everyday life. It is based on fundamental concepts constituting a Mesoamerican cosmovision that are today as much a part of everyday life as they were five hundred years ago.

The epilogue is anecdotal, yet it shows that this system is as resonant today with the ethos of Mesoamerican peoples as it was for their ancestors. This is how a practitioner with knowledge and compassion can help friends and villagers to grapple with the changes of everyday life. This is the burden that I took on when I agreed to learn Doña Rubia's tradition, and this is the burden that I carry with me to this day. I view this book as part of my burden.

Ben Fierro © 2003

CHAPTER ONE

EARTH AND SKY, BODY AND SOUL

The Dialogics of Life on the Earth and Life in the Most Holy Earth

IN SAN MARTÍN ZINACAPAN in the Sierra de Puebla, life of the earth, in the earth, and on the earth is animated by the same forces. Through these forces, people seek to maintain a coherent, cohesive view of the relationship between humankind, the cosmos, and the natural world—a coherent ecology of spirit. This delicate balance of the human spirit maintains the health and well-being of villagers and is an essential part of the social and ideological framework that makes life whole. This chapter will attempt to describe in a coherent way the basic elements of the beliefs and practices underlying this system.

As Bateson has noted, "A description can never resemble the thing described" (Bateson and Bateson 1988: 151). It is in fact a mapping of the fabric of life. The social fabric that is constituted by these basic features of the cosmos weaves together concepts of the earth, body, and soul. This is a description that links together the three levels of the cosmos—*ilhuicac*, *talticpac*, and *talocan*; the sky, the earth, and the underworld—with three aspects of the soul: *notonal*, *noyollo*, and *nonagual*; my breath soul, my heart soul, and my animal alter ego.

Although the current cosmological principles of the people of San Martín Zinacapan have no direct link or relationship to those of their ancestors the Toltecs,[1] or, more remotely, the Aztecs, the concepts are nevertheless based on the same underlying Mesoamerican principles. There are no direct links between the highly codified cosmovision of the Aztec Empire at the time of the Spanish conquest and that of the village of San Martín Zinacapan today, yet there is an eerie similarity, almost a mapping.

The similarity of these systems should be quite obvious to anyone familiar with ethnohistorical sources concerned with cosmovision. First, it is due to the fundamental homology of basic principles that relate humankind to the natural and social world in Mesoamerica. These fundamental principles have remained constant for centuries, perhaps millennia. They are strongly based on astute observation of the natural world and humankind's relationship to that world (McKeever Furst 1995). Second, this system of beliefs is held far more extensively than in just this single village. The similarities found in this system are based on the way curers, the priest-shamans of the Most Holy Earth, *talocan,* followers of the 'good path,' *cualli ohti,* are trained. This system of apprenticeship and practice can be traced back at least as far as the messianic movements of the sixteenth and seventeenth centuries. The tumultuous period just after the Spanish conquest is when traditional religion, confronted with imposed Catholicism and mass conversions, became a separate and distinct covert system of beliefs satisfying basic needs and serving as a personal and private form of resistance to the newly imposed order (Aramoni 1990).

Since then, new realities and traditional knowledge has been synthesized into this system in a way that is satisfying to villagers in their everyday life. It is not a syncretic mixing of concepts of old and new, but rather an ongoing dialectic that interprets new realities in terms of a traditional ethos (B. Tedlock 1983). Neither is this a system of canonical texts and doctrines followed since the sixteenth century and before. It is rather based on a system of apprenticeship, training, and practice that is passed from one specialist to the next. It is a relationship of pupil and teacher, apprentice and master, linked through the centuries in lineages or schools that have not only perpetuated traditional beliefs but protected them from interference by the outside world. This system effectively synthesizes beliefs about both the social and natural phenomena of the everyday world on the basis of commonsense knowledge.

The modern manifestation of this system remains a highly special-ized body of knowledge. My intention is to show this as a clear and coherent modern system in its own right. Where I have drawn on sources based on the study of Classical Aztec concepts, pre-Columbian cosmo-vision, I have generally drawn on modern interpretive work that is designed to shed light on the present system rather than on the vast and often con-fusing ethnohistorical sources.

In order to understand this system, it is necessary to begin with a brief introduction to the three aspects of the cosmos and three aspects of the human soul that interact to maintain and sustain life on the earth. This is followed by an overview of the relationships that villagers maintain in public and private religion with the Most Holy Earth, *talocan*. Under-standing the human soul, its role in dreams and in maintaining the well-being of villagers, is a complex matter. Thus the final part of this chapter consists of a more detailed account of the soul and its relation to the world.

THREE LEVELS OF THE COSMOS

There are three realms of the cosmos with which humankind must inter-act in body and spirit. Humankind inhabits the earth between two potent realms of the supernatural. The sky, *ilhuicac,* is the realm of heat, light, and day. The sky is the unattainable heaven of the saints, virgins, and Jesucristo; it is the source of light, *nexti,* also glossed as *gracia* or 'grace,' which makes life possible on the surface of the earth, providing heat and the spark of life that animates body and soul.

The sky is also the primary focus of public religious activities that bind the village together in the great public festivals, such as that of the patron saint of the village, San Martín. These great public celebrations link kin and fictive kin, mobilizing lineages and social networks that are an essential part of the fabric of social life in the village.

The Most Holy Earth, *talocan,* sustains mankind both literally and fig-uratively. It is a realm of darkness and night, yet it provides the sustenance of humankind, the fecundity of the earth, the life-giving moisture on which all living things depend. This is the underworld of darkness and night yet also of growth and sustenance. This is the world of the traditions of the ancestors. It is the primary focus of private family-based beliefs and traditions. It is everywhere within the earth, a dark mirror of the waking world of everyday life.

The surface of the earth, *talticpac,* maintains the essential separation between the two opposing realms of the supernatural. The activities of humankind on the earth maintain, or seek to maintain, based on a coherent natural philosophy, the fundamental order of the cosmos. As in the pre-Columbian world (López Austin 1994), humankind lives *ipan in talticpac,* between earth, *talocan,* and *ilhuicac,* sky—light and darkness, savage and civilized space.

Three Souls

The fundamental order that humankind seeks to maintain with the cosmos is the same as the fundamental balance, or equilibrium, that must be maintained for life itself to continue on the surface of the earth. There are three fundamental aspects of the human soul that must be maintained in harmony with the natural, social, and cosmological worlds for life on earth.

An individual has three elements that are part of the soul: *notonal,* which is often glossed as 'my soul' or 'breath'; *noyollo,* which is the heart and physical body; and *nonagual,* which is the most problematic aspect of the soul, often glossed as 'my other' or the darker, savage aspects of an individual and personality. All three aspects must at all times be maintained in a proper and harmonious balance in the individual, as well as in the social, natural, and supernatural worlds, or the individual risks illness and even death.

Actual naming of at least one of these aspects of the soul may be arbitrary (Signorini and Lupo 1989), and few individuals agree completely on the nature of the various aspects of the soul. Just as Western theologians have debated the nature of the soul for centuries (McKeever Furst 1995: 14–16), so villagers are perplexed by the nature of the soul. Problems concerning the nature of the soul in Mesoamerica are legion (López Austin 1980: 221–318). Suffice it to say that there are problems that are semantic in nature, social in nature, and epistemological in nature. Concepts concerning the soul are the province of specialists, yet they concern everyone and are essential for maintaining the physical, psychological, and social health of the community.

In an agrarian society that can ill afford the luxury of specialists in dedicated academies to debate issues such as the nature of the soul, this knowledge must have a specific practical role in society. Specialists in the human soul are traditional healers, *tepahtini,* who, through a fundamentally practical knowledge, seek to maintain the balance of all three aspects of the soul for the maintenance of life on the earth. Such individuals are curers, priests of the earth, technicians of the sacred, shaman-dreamers.[2] They are the specialists whose intimate knowledge must be relied upon in matters of tradition. The traditions of the ancestors constitute the philosophy, cosmology, psychology, sociology, and anthropology of the community. Curers use a liberal dose of tradition to maintain the harmony of the soul and the health of their clients.

These specialists maintain direct personal contacts through their dreams with the realm of the supernatural, the underworld of the ancestors, *talocan.* Such individuals bear a tradition, which they view as a burden, for their fellow villagers, which seeks to maintain humankind's position in the cosmos between earth and sky. Their tradition is not taken lightly and must be passed on to others before death, or their own souls will forever wander the reaches of darkness.

Life, from the viewpoint of Sanmartinos, depends on a balance, an equilibrium. An individual who maintains this balance of life is said to live well, *cualli nehnemi,* or according to the traditional ways of the ancestors. Such an individual is viewed as a traditional, moral person who is an essential part of the fabric of society, someone who recognizes that the social, natural, and cosmological orders must be maintained in constant balance for life to continue. This ecology of the human spirit is essential for everyday life in the Sierra de Puebla today, as it was for the ancestors of these people centuries ago.

It is not an ecology of the mind à la Bateson (1974), but rather of the spirit (Bateson and Bateson 1988: 142), that must be maintained within the natural, social, and cosmological orders. Balance, or harmony, is viewed in this situation as essential for the production and reproduction of life on the earth. The role of the shaman, the priest or priestess of the Most Holy Earth, the curer, is to maintain this harmony of the spirit, through prayer, ritual, and direct personal contact with the supernatural in dreams.

The relationship of humankind to the natural and supernatural worlds in which life exists has in fact changed little in the nearly five hundred years since the Spanish conquest. There are new crops—coffee for cash instead of corn for life—but the ideology of a corn-based economy of subsistence agriculture has changed little (Sandstrom 1991).

In San Martín this is expressed in the following way:

Well, now we plant coffee, we harvest the coffee,
we dry the coffee, we sell the coffee.
but, it is with corn that we live, we eat.
The holy earth nourishes us with tortillas,
the holy earth sprouts the new corn.
It is our life.[3]

The fundamental contradictions of ethnic enclaves in a regional and national state and economy (Boege 1988) have also changed little, as numerous groups have held power. New ideologies are easily adapted to the realities of traditional concepts. The utopias of the ancients are always available as models for today (Wolf 1987). A new synthesis of the world can be easily formulated from the traditional concepts that have formed the basic precepts of life since time immemorial (B. Tedlock 1983).

Changes in circumstance and ideology are rapidly absorbed, as was the French invasion of the region. The invasion is but a memory, now reflected in some aspects of the cuisine and a few loanwords from the French. There is no present memory of the invasion; it has become a part of someone else's history. Little has changed despite vast changes in the nation (Bonfil 1990). The values, concepts, metaphors, and meanings that make life coherent in San Martín Zinacapan have remained since long before the French invasion, the advent of coffee as a cash crop, the construction of the new *presidencia* and the new school, the reconstruction of the church, and the advent of Catholic Action. And they will remain long after history is assimilated and disappears behind the veil of myth and tradition.

The Most Holy Earth

If we are to understand the underlying concepts that constitute Mesoamerican cosmovision, we must understand that Tlaloc, a fundamental deity in the Aztec world, was far more than a deity of rain and water. The powers of Tlaloc over the rains and water are but a single aspect of this deity. Unfortunately many individuals, from sixteenth-century chroniclers (Torquemada 1943: II, 72; Motolinía 1971: 51–67) to modern academics (Seler 1963) have persisted in this error.

Tlaloc is not a rain deity. Tlaloc is the earth. He/she is the deified embodiment of the earth in the pre-Columbian pantheon. As such, Tlaloc represents some of the most ancient and fundamental principles of Mesoamerican cosmovision. Tlaloc, as the earth, is the foundation on which such religious concepts rest.

As Thelma D. Sullivan (1972) stated in the introduction to her paper *Tlaloc: A new etymological interpretation of the God's name and what it reveals of his essence and nature,* which she presented at the 40th International Congress of Americanists in Rome: "He was the fecundator of the earth upon which all humankind depended for its sustenance, its existence: he was the moisture that made the earth fructify" (1972: 213). Thelma Sullivan's etymological analysis of the meaning of Tlaloc's name is an example of the power of the philological method that she employed throughout her work. As she pointed out: "since the names of Nahuatl gods are literally or figuratively a description of their nature, it would appear that Tlaloc was essentially an earth god" (1972: 217). Although several scholars have pointed out certain problems with Sullivan's etymology[4], she remains fundamentally correct in her interpretation.

Numerous modern scholars now recognize Tlaloc as an earth deity (including Heyden 1975; Broda 1987; Aveni et al. 1988). This is in fundamental agreement with current ethnographic evidence from the Sierra de Puebla showing that Sullivan's analysis of the deity was correct. Tlaloc is both male and female as were many, if not most, pre-Columbian deities. Tlaloc was the earth but also the provider of moisture on which life depends.

Tlaloc did not die with the Spanish conquest. Such a potent concept as the fecundator of the earth and sustainer of humankind has not yet been purged from the minds of the conquered. As late as the nineteenth century on Tlaloc's sacred mountain just outside of Mexico City, new-born children were sacrificed to him to assure crops (Barlow cited in Wicke and Horcasitas 1957: 86). Tlaloc took refuge deep in the unconscious of the conquered, and today, in some remote regions, mentions of his domain are common (Reyes 1976; Taggart 1983; Aramoni 1990; Signorini and Lupo 1989; Lupo 1995).

In the Sierra de Puebla, *talocan* (as Tlalocan, the domain of Tlaloc, is referred to in the Sierra Nahuat of San Martín Zinacapan) is very much a part of the everyday life of the villagers (Knab 1991; 1995). For a few knowledgeable curers, the essence and nature of Taloc, as he/she is called in the Sierra de Puebla, is, or at least was, a vital concern. As Broda (1987: 106) suggested, "This basic symbolism of water, the earth, the sky, and the sun seems to reveal certain basic philosophical concepts that have ancient roots in Mesoamerican culture." This basic Mesoamerican philosophy is alive and well in the Sierra de Puebla today.

Beliefs in *talocan* in San Martín vary from vague to concise and elaborate, yet most individuals will agree with the statement *talocan talmanic,* '*talocan* extends throughout the earth,' whether or not they have concise notions of the underworld of their ancestors. The nature and essence of the concepts that constitute private household religion are unique. The meaning of *taloc* today can be seen through the words, prayers, and tales of the people of the Sierra de Puebla. Specialists who journey regularly to this realm of the supernatural in their dreams constitute a living tradition that was thought to have died with the Spanish conquest.

The relationships between individuals in the Sierra de Puebla are the same as the relationships between humankind and the cosmos. They connect parents and children, ritual kinspeople or *compadres,* members of the religious hierarchy, the *mayordomo* and the *fiscales* or *topiles.* Life on the earth, life in the earth, and life of the sky is based on the same fundamental types of relationship, which structure the way people view relationships with the natural and supernatural worlds.

The types of relationships that are maintained are reciprocal, or at least have the expectation of reciprocity. Aiding a relation or fellow villager in arranging the immensely complicated festivals of the patron saint, with money or labor for example, puts the onus of obligation on the other to provide some type of aid in the future. With relatives and especially with ritual kin, *compadres,* this reciprocity is even more important for the relationship. It is in fact required. In other cases, it is hoped for and expected but by no means obligatory.

Basic social relationships are analogous to those relationships between humankind and the supernatural, which are also viewed as reciprocal. There are two subtly different types of reciprocal relationships with the supernatural that are common in San Martín: maintenance and sustenance. Maintenance is viewed as a continuous and ongoing relationship occurring constantly through time. The people of San Martín maintain their families, their church, the festivals of the saints, and their relationships with the Most Holy Earth.

An individual must also provide something in exchange for sustenance, the nourishment needed for life. Relationships based on sustenance are reciprocal, but they last only as long as an individual lives or a particular event is sustained. A *mayordomo* sustains a festival for his term in office, and in exchange he benefits from the status, position, and extended social network resulting from his labors and expenditures. A household sustains children until they move out and start their own households. Offerings from the new harvest symbolically sustain the Most Holy Earth, and the moisture of the underworld sustains humankind's life on the earth. Sustenance is a nurturing relationship that is fundamental to social, natural, and supernatural interaction.

Permission is another category fundamental to relationships in San Martín. All features of the social and natural world are controlled by someone or something. Their use requires permission, either from an individual or a supernatural being. Permission must be obtained before an individual can legitimately claim benefit from his or her actions in everyday life. Permission is sought through elegant and florid discourses, supplications, and prayers that seek to cajole (Lupo 1995) and convince the parties concerned to grant permission. Permission must be obtained of the Most Holy Earth before cultivating it. Permission must be obtained of one's fellow villagers before becoming part of the civil or religious hierarchy. Permission is obtained from the supernatural in the same way that it is obtained from one's fellow villagers—with offerings and supplications. The granting of permission implies some type of mutual benefit that is gained, some specific form of reciprocity.

The fundamental goal of both public and private religious practice in San Martín is to maintain the cosmic equilibrium essential for life. Public religion in San Martín focuses on the cult of the saints, the virgins, and Jesucristo, the supernaturals of the sky who provide the earth with their holy light or *nexti*. It is their holy light, equated with 'grace,' that keeps the powers of darkness, the lords of the underworld, *talocan*, at bay, thus sustaining life on earth. Private household religion focuses on the family altar, the traditions of the ancestors, and the Most Holy Earth, *talocan*, which sustains humankind with its life-giving moisture.

The center of public religious activities is the church of San Martín in the center of town. The church is not only the physical center of the town, but it is also the metaphorical center of social activity in San Martín. Public social life centering on the political and religious hierarchies of the cults of the state and the saints maintain the public order and harmony essential for everyday life in the town. As an individual ascends in these public hierarchies, the number of reciprocal relationships that are maintained with fellow villagers and the supernaturals of the sky increase. Each office is considered to grant an individual a certain amount of 'holy light' or 'grace' that will help to obtain the next office. Likewise, each office is seen as a metaphorical plant:

> Each one flowers and is good
> It bears fruit of another 'position'
> But if it should wither   if it should die
> there are no more.

The metaphoric plant thrives in the light of the sky, *ilhuicac,* and with the nourishment of the holy earth, *talocan.*

In this way, public religion maintains the public system of social order and organization that is essential to social, political, and economic cooperation. Private or household religion that focuses on the cult of the Most Holy Earth, on the other hand, is centered on the individual, the family, the household altar, kin relationships, health, and the human soul. This essential aspect of religious practice also seeks to maintain the harmony for life on the earth. Public and private beliefs are complementary systems that both have as their essential goal the maintenance of cosmological order essential for life on earth. Feeding the underworld and glorifying the sky both maintain and sustain the activities of everyday life.

Disease and death are the result of imbalances between the soul and its natural, social, and supernatural environments. The primary nexus of private or household religion is the human soul. Traditional curers, *tepahtini,* seek to resolve imbalances and restore the soul to its natural state within the cosmological order via various rituals, offerings, and supplications. The traditional curer maintains health and thus human life on the earth. An individual whose soul is not maintained in the proper state of equilibrium with the social, natural, and supernatural environments will become ill and eventually die if balance is not restored. A Sanmartino's soul that is not in balance with the cosmos and its fundamental order will soon transpose its owner from the land of the living on the surface of the earth, *in talticpac,* to the underworld of the ancestors, *talocan.* The dead of San Martín reside in the earth; they are the ancestors memorialized beneath household altars.

Every home in San Martín has an altar. It may be no more than a few pictures of the saints above a table. It may be an elaborate central feature of the home festooned with hundreds of images, paper flowers, fresh flowers, dried and dead flowers, elaborate foil decorations, popular representations of Christ, the Virgin, or innumerable saints, old calendar art, photos of relatives or friends, and elaborate tissue cutouts.

The altar is a representation of the cosmos. Above it, in the realm of the sky, *ilhuicac,* are the saints, Christ, the virgins, etc. On the surface of the altar, which represents the surface of the earth, *talticpac,* are offerings, perhaps some fresh flowers and probably a votive candle. Beneath the altar in the realm of the underworld, *talocan,* are relics of the ancestors; pre-Columbian pot shards or obsidian flakes, hair or clothing of departed relatives, and blackened censers which are either buried in the earth or kept in a trunk.

The household altar is the central focus of private religious functions, household celebrations, and curing rituals. A trained practitioner will rearrange a family altar before beginning to pray and cure to assure that everything is in the proper order reflecting the cosmos. At times, elaborate offerings are placed on the altar, beneath the altar, or on shelves above the altar. During curing rituals, these offerings are symbolically moved from one realm of the cosmos to another. Offerings for the earth at harvest time can be placed before a cave, one of the entryways into the underworld, as payment to the lords of the earth for their bounty, or beneath the household altar, signifying that they are intended for the Most Holy Earth.

For curings, memorial services, the taking of new *compadres,* and almost all other household celebrations, the altar is the central focus of ritual. It reiterates the structure of the cosmos and allows practitioners to symbolically manipulate the relationships among the three realms of the cosmos. By manipulating offerings, prayers, and rituals in front of the altar the practitioner seeks to restore, maintain, or sustain essential aspects of the cosmological order and harmony essential for life on earth. It is before

the altar that a practitioner seeks permission of the supernatural, or jus-
tice, or pays the earth its due. It is also before the altar that relationships
of *compadrazgo* are cemented, offerings for the departed are made, and
newborns presented 'in the holy light' to the world of the living. The altar
is the central focus of household religion, where people seek to maintain
the delicate balance of the soul essential for life on the earth between
the sky and the underworld.

THE SOUL: ON THE EARTH, IN THE EARTH, AND IN THE SKY

The soul is the central animic entity that gives an individual life and char-
acter. For the Sanmartino, a soul consists of three parts, overlapping and
problematic in nature as we will see, but fulfilling most of the same functions of the Western soul as well as many more. The soul itself is a model
of the cosmos based on and in the human body (López Austin 1980),
and as Davíd Carrasco (1990) points out, this is part of the world-center-
ing basis of Mesoamerican religion that is seen in all things, from the
layout of ceremonial centers to the nature of the deities.

Jill Leslie McKeever Furst's magnificent work *The Natural History of the
Soul in Ancient Mexico* (1995) provides an inkling into the complexity of
Mesoamerican concepts concerning the human soul. Such concepts in
Mesoamerica are in fact based on commonsense knowledge of the natural world extended to the supernatural. This is a fundamental point of
McKeever Furst's work with which I am in complete accord. Her work
shows the immense range in beliefs concerning the soul engendered by
the Native American propensity toward astute observation of the natural
world and also questions our Western tendency to subdivide and classify
such esoteric concepts as those concerning the human soul (McKeever
Furst 1995: 173–84).

Many distinct aspects of the human soul can be, and often are, collapsed into one single aspect of the soul and classified under a single term.
This is a semantic process that is as common in Mesoamerica today as it
probably was at the time of the Spanish conquest and long before. Unlike
Western peoples, whose religious wars scar their history, many Mesoamericans, to paraphrase Will Rogers, "never met a religion they didn't
like." What seem conflicting and contradictory beliefs to the Western
mind are of little concern in Mesoamerica.

It is not at all unusual to find a traditional shaman who is also a member of Catholic Action and even a member of another evangelical sect. For this reason, concepts concerning such esoteric beliefs as those surrounding the nature of the soul are nebulous and fluid. It is we, as Westerners, who seek neat schemes with traditional labels for these esoteric concepts. Mesoamerican metaphors and concepts are often bipolar, defining an entity by its differences and contrasts. Such vastly different semantic processes contribute heavily to the load of confusion heaped on such concepts as the soul.

There are at least three levels of semantic confusion concerning the nature of the soul that must be considered. First, at the time of the conquest, the friars—though sophisticated in theology—were burdened with the views of Spanish renaissance humanism, the Reformation, and Spain's radical retreat into faith and completely lacked the techniques necessary to analyze Mesoamerican concepts of the soul. There was never a treatise produced on the Mesoamerican concepts of the soul. Modern scholars (López Austin 1980; McKeever Furst 1995) have long labored to understand the nature of the Aztec soul, and the results have been impressive, despite serious pitfalls.

Second, the terms used for different aspects of the soul were probably thickets of metaphor and homophony, as they are today, which made Mesoamericans value them even more. For as Alfredo López Austin (1980: 228) pointed out, "Many times, the value of a metaphor is found in its polyvalent quality and double meanings that play on words to create a poetic image and also express a deeper concept." The semantic confusion that this has created has been multiplied many times over by constant reanalysis and synthesis (B. Tedlock 1983) of such concepts that are central to Mesoamerican religious beliefs. Terms and concepts of the nature of the human soul in modern contexts and in Classic Aztec must be carefully compared and contrasted at the semantic level if we are to understand the real meaning of concepts of the soul in the larger context of everyday life.

Another and perhaps less well-known source of semantic confusion is in the realm of multiculturalism that exists in Mesoamerica today, which probably existed in pre-Columbian times. Folk Spanish concepts concerning such basic points of Mesoamerican beliefs as *nagualism* (Brinton 1894; Foster 1944; Villa Rojas 1963; Aguirre Beltran 1983) cross back and forth from indigenous to mestizo worlds as easily as their members change from indigenous to mestizo clothes, to business suits. Concepts cross ethnic boundaries throughout the multicultural world that is Mesoamerica in unpredictable ways. This adds a level of semantic confusion that requires an extensive knowledge of native languages and beliefs to clear up.

Much, if not most, of the material presented here would have never been uncovered without the consistent and constant use of Nahuat as a primary means of communication. Terms for such things as the underworld of the ancestors, *talocan,* are glossed in Spanish as the *infierno,* 'hell,' or as *la santisima tierra,* 'the Most Holy Earth.' Quite a difference!

Nahuat also distinguishes between the possessed form of an animal alter ego, *nonagual,* 'my nagual,' my animal alter ego; and *nagualli,* 'the witch.' Likewise, *tonalli* is glossed as 'day,' whereas *notonal* is 'my soul,' 'my fate,' and also by implication the animal alter ego, '*mi otro,*' with whom the individual shares the *itonal,*[5] as well as 'my breath.' Such distinctions become crucial in deciding on a name for the third and unnamed aspect of the soul. In Spanish, most Sanmartinos describe a *nagualli* as a powerful witch and will describe the *miquitagat* or *ejecacihuat,* horrific manifestations of the underworld lords, when pressed, as the prototypic *nagualli.* *Nonagual* will be glossed as '*mi animal,*' '*mi otro,*' or '*el otro yo*'—'my animal,' 'my other,' or 'my other self'—and equated with the shadow, *ecahuil,* which is also equated with the *tonal.* The shadow is the counterpart of the *tonal,* its dark alternate (Signorini and Lupo, 1989: 77), thus also another aspect of what I have called the *nagual.*

There are common tales of revolutionary and political leaders endowed with the power of a *nagualli* or witch in Spanish, mestizo folk beliefs, which are often adapted into Nahuat folklore, further confusing the matter. The use of Spanish as a trade language for discussing esoteric concepts is not only confusing but usually counterproductive and frustrating for all involved. It almost never results in a worthwhile formulation.

There seems to be general agreement that there are three basic aspects to the soul (López Austin 1980; González Torres 1976; Signorini and Lupo 1989; McKeever Furst 1995) in both Classic Aztec and Modern Aztec concepts. Where disagreement lies is in the naming of these aspects of the soul and their exact nature, rather than in their tripartite structure. Long discussions with both Rubia and Inocente, my primary men-

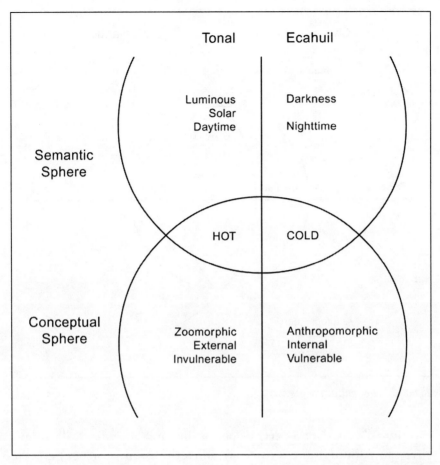

Figure 1. Semantic and conceptual aspects of the soul (after Signorini and Lupo 1989).

tors in this esoteric field who often did not even agree among themselves, have led me to the particular notion that I have chosen. For others, different considerations have been more important than the ones I have chosen for specific semantic reasons (Signorini and Lupo 1989).[6] (See Figure 1 for a basic diagram of the semantic differentiation of distinctive aspects of the soul from Signorini and Lupo [1989: 77].)

Signorini and Lupo (1989: 77) are trying in this diagram to distinguish just the semantic and conceptual differences between the *tonal* and the *ecahuil,* or 'shadow,' which I have chosen to associate with the *nagual.* This is the alternative aspect of the soul, its 'shadow,' which is associated with

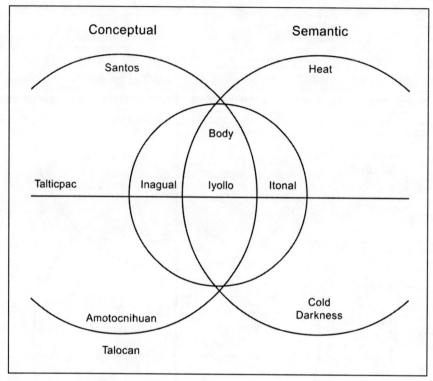

Conceptual   Semantic

Santos   Heat

Body

Talticpac   Inagual   Iyollo   Itonal

Cold
Darkness

Amotocnihuan

Talocan

Figure 2. The soul in the cosmos.

the savage, cold, dark aspects of personality and an individual's animal
alter ego. Although the terms may differ, the essential structure is the
same as that I have described with the addition of hot and cold aspects
of disease, which are probably aspects of pre-Columbian beliefs (Ortiz de
Montellano, 1990).

The tripartite structure remains the same in nearly all discussions,
though its content may vary. Some aspects of the soul may be inverted
in areas that are separated by short distances.[7] Nevertheless, as is indicated
in Figure 2, the range of interaction in both the conceptual and semantic
spheres is analogous to Signorini and Lupo's (1989: 77) model but rotated
ninety degrees.

Although labels and names can vary considerably, there is a certain
heterodox unity in the basic concepts of the soul that integrate three
aspects of the soul with concepts of the sky, earth, and underworld. Figures 2 and 3 integrate concepts of all three aspects of the soul with con-

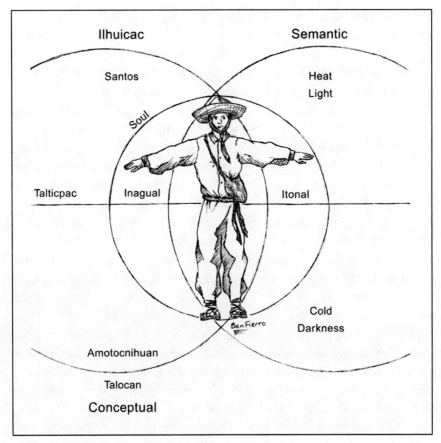

Figure 3. Body and soul in the conceptual world.

cepts of the earth, sky, and underworld. I have chosen to illustrate the three aspects of the soul integrated into the overall structure of earth, sky, and underworld. The *yollo* remains on the surface of the earth or is buried in the earth when an individual dies. The *tonal* can wander in dreams to the sky and underworld but is essentially part of the individual through-out his or her life on the surface of the earth. The *nagual,* or animal alter ego, shares the *tonal,* or in Signorini and Lupo's sense, the 'shadow' or cool savage part of the *tonal,* with an individual. The *nagual* is kept by the lord of animals in the underworld but may escape and wander either the under-world or the surface of the earth. Avian *naguals* can also wander the skies to a limited degree. Figure 2 integrates all of these aspects of the soul and the cosmos along a horizontal line, whereas Figure 3 integrates humankind into a system that is essentially analogous to Signorini and Lupo's distinction, albeit with considerable additional material integrated into it.

In his discussion of the Classic Aztec souls and their relation to concepts of the body, Alfredo López Austin (1980: 257) points out that, while there is good documentary evidence for the descriptions of the *tonal* and the *teyolia,* the 'heart soul,' the term for the third aspect of the soul is in fact rather arbitrary. He derives the name, rather circuitously by his own admission (López Austin 1980: 258), from a Chortí term, possibly from Spanish, *hijillo,* which is almost homophonous with *ihiyotl. Ihiyotl* describes the foul eminence from the dead (Wisdom 1940) and an aspect of the soul for other Mayan groups, as well, that is closely related to (in fact, borrowed from) the Nahua. López Austin's association of this aspect of the soul with the liver is well reasoned (López Austin 1980: 259). Naming the third aspect of the soul is a daunting task even for native practitioners.

Evidence from sixteenth-century dictionaries of Classic Aztec is likewise confusing concerning this third aspect of the soul, masking the nature of the concept and making it appear similar to the breath soul that is generally equated with the *tonal* and heart soul, *teyolia.* This aspect of the soul is, however, a foul or disgusting eminence from the body quite unlike the breath, though easily confused with it as McKeever Furst (1995) points out. In a modern context, it is almost always associated very closely with witchcraft, the dark or savage aspects of personality, and the cold humors.

McKeever Furst (1995: 160–73) derives this aspect of the soul from direct observation of the dead: the rather foul aroma that envelops them and is equated with decomposition and also creates methane gas, which produces the swamp glow, or *ignus fatus.* This does fit with the rather disparate definitions of the term, and it is in accord with the physical evidence, which would be apparent to people living on the shores of a stagnant lakebed as were the Aztecs of Tenochtitlan, present-day Mexico City.

The great advantage of McKeever Furst's derivation of the three aspects of the soul for the Mexica is that it relies directly on observable phenomena (McKeever Furst 1995). Aztec souls were defined in terms of experience rather than theology.

Even today, the nature of the soul is a matter of practical speculation, rather than theological dogma. Both Rubia and Inocente spent long hours discussing this nature of the soul and speculating on it in seemingly contradictory ways. Inocente once commented that:

> Well, my *nagual* is my other thing, that thing that is bad, it is not good. It lives there in the cave in the darkness. It is cold. Maybe it is like death. When I feel a cold spot on someone I think that maybe there is something that is not right with their *nagual,* but it could be an evil wind too that's got 'em. If it's cold, it's like death, but if your *nagual* dies then, poaf! You're dead, unless you've got another one of those things. I've got plenty of them! I'll show 'em to you, but don't say anything about them, or they'll know you're a witch. All of 'em are a little bit more on the candle [a bit more added to life], but they're cold. There's death in every one of them.

The practitioners with whom I worked had disagreements concerning details of the form, shape, or nature of the underworld and the soul as well. Rubia would often explain a particular aspect of her notion of the soul, such as the relationship between the breath and the *tonal,* and then correct herself the next day after considering the matter further. Concepts of the nature of the soul were never, for the practitioners, fixed doctrines, but rather flexible metaphors adapted to the experiences of everyday life in the practice of curing.

My own interpretation of this is based on the practical aspect of curing, the real and symbolic manipulation of the soul within the realities of everyday life. Practical knowledge and use of concepts of the soul in curing, dreaming, and even witchcraft lead me to a slightly different view of the nature of the soul, which is, however, in accordance with that of McKeever Furst (1995), Signorini and Lupo (1989), López Austin (1980), González Torres (1976), and others.

The names for the three aspects of the soul, the *itonal,* the *iyollo,* and the *inagual,* are not arbitrarily chosen. Linguistically all three are what are called bound forms, i.e., none of them can appear without possession unless they're radically altered semantically. They must be mine, *no-,* yours, *mo-,* or hers, *i-,* integral parts of the individual's spirit. As bound forms they are aspects of the soul, but unbound, as independent substantives, they are concepts as disparate as the words for witch, heart, heat, and day. The internal logic of this system shows that it is derived from experience in everyday life, and it is in fact today part of a practical system for healing the body and spirit.

Yollot: *The Internal Force, the Heart*

The *iyollo* is the internal animic force that is directly associated with the heart and the blood. Concepts concerning this aspect of the soul are the clearest and most easily accessible. One's heart is the center of animic force that gives the body life. It must remain with the individual until death in its central position in the body. The *iyollo* is the part of the soul that is consumed by the earth, *talocan,* upon an individual's death (McKeever Furst 1995: 128). Life of the body and the *iyollo* are synonymous. Blood is the outward manifestation of the *iyollo,* and its ability to clot and solidify indicates a natural progression from the moving and flowing of life to death. Both the constant movement of the blood and breath are characteristics of the *iyollo.*

Metaphorically, one who is of good heart, *cualli yollotzin* or *yolcualli,* is strong, brave, and intelligent. One with a destroyed heart *yolpolihuiz,* is mad, disturbed, or prone to fits. Individuals not complying with particular obligations are prone to a watery heart, *ayollot,* as for example when a curer, *tepahtini,* does not pass on his or her particular skills, or when a *mayordomo* does not properly arrange a particular saint or virgin's celebration. A watery heart is a slothful or lazy heart.[8] The heart can also be referred to as the seed of life or grain of corn, *yoltagolli.*

The botanical metaphor in San Martín is one of the organizing metaphors of great potency in the town (Knab 1984). Life is seen as analogous to the growth of plants, and the heart, *iyollo,* the center of life in the body, in particular to the planting and growth of a grain of corn. The plant is the metaphorical body, and the grains of corn from which the crop springs forth are the heart. The obvious similarity in form of a grain of corn to the heart is also well known, as are many anatomical similarities of the plant.[9]

The *iyollo* is not strictly the physical heart, but is what would be called the internal animic force distributed throughout the body, analogous to, but not equated with, the blood. It is also the *iyollo* that a curer is checking when pulsing a client's body, feeling for the movement of blood and heat. This is an indication of inhabitations, which can cause dislocations of the soul.

The *iyollo* can be displaced by the 'evil winds,' *mal aires, ahmocualli ehecat,* which include the winds of the earth, the night winds, and the winds of death. It can also be displaced by an envious glance, the evil eye that may also cause a 'magical fright,' *susto, nemouhtil.* The presence of either type of displacement of the *iyollo* will cause subtle changes in the temperature of a client's body and strange movements in the blood that can actually be felt. These kinds of things can be massaged out of the body, or sucked out, metaphorically restoring the *iyollo* to its central position and bringing the soul back into balance.

Several common forms of witchcraft seek to displace the *iyollo.* A witch can send an evil wind or can metaphorically cover his victim's heart by burning a candle upside down. In this case, the candle is seen as the heart, *iyollo,* and the flame as the *itonal,* and the two consume each other. These relatively benign forms of witchcraft can be combined with potent techniques of poisoning and the transmission of particular diseases in ways that make them quite effective and deadly. San Martín is a town known throughout the region for witchcraft (Ross 1950).

Tonal: *Distinguishing Fate, Day, and Sun*

The *itonal* is a far more problematic aspect of the soul. It is often glossed in Spanish as *el suspiro* or *soplo,* as well as 'soul,' *anima,* but it is much more than a breath soul. It is the loosely held aspect of the soul that travels in dreams and can be knocked or scared out of the individual and lost, causing sickness and death. The *itonal* is the life force that brings heat to the body. It is responsible for the individual's intelligence and cunning.

Tonalli is day; *totonic* is hot; *tonalan* is dusk or sunset. *Notonal,* as an aspect of the soul, is a number of different things at once. It is referred to as the cause of one's shadow, *ecahuil,* or the shadow itself, and can be looked at as the cool, dark aspect of the soul. It can also be looked at as the shaman's familiar, as Signorini and Lupo (1989: 77) point out. The shaman and familiar share this aspect of the soul. *Notonal huan itonal,* 'my tonal and his tonal,' are born and die at the same instant, yet the familiar is called *nonagual,* the 'animal alter ego.' The confusion here is not simply semantic, and it is not simply a difference of interpretation on the part of anthropologists and native practitioners. As McKeever Furst (1995: 184) notes, "The animal companion deserves an entire book of its own."

There are several distinct notions or concepts collapsed into this term. Some overlap with concepts associated with the *iyollo* and others with the *inagual*. Some of the points of conceptual confusion result from the fact that the individual and the animal alter ego share breath and destiny associated with the *itonal*. Others from the fact that the *tonal* is detachable from both the individual and the animal alter ego yet essential for continued life. The intelligence or cunning of both is associated with the *itonal*.

As Yolotl González Torres (1976) has shown, the *tonal* is the life force that animated all things in the pre-Columbian view. The *tonal* is the animic force that gives the individual the spark of life, the heat of the living, distinguishing him or her from the dead.

The *itonal* is the detachable animic force. It carries with it an individual's destiny in the earth, on the earth, and in the sky. This potent and fundamental notion of the *itonal* is what in fact gives it such prominence and makes its nature appear problematic; the *itonal* has a multiplicity of distinct attributes that practitioners must learn to manipulate to maintain the equilibrium of the human soul.

In the Sierra Norte de Puebla, the term *tonal* has shifted to mean the animal alter ego, for the Nahuat term for that entity, *inagual*, has shifted in folk belief to imply a powerful and evil witch, *nagualli*, which is in fact quite different from the individual's animal alter ego, *nonagual*. This is a semantic shift that is no longer in accord with the term's original meaning.

The *itonal* is the part of the soul that is most loosely held. It can be easily stolen by a witch or by inhabitants of the underworld who would keep it in the underworld, where it would die without benefit of the light of day, *nexti*, or 'grace.' The individual will not survive long without the *itonal*. A *tonal* needs the heat and light of day for full health. The *itonal*, unlike the *iyollo*, may live on after an individual has died and returned to the Most Holy Earth, *talocan*. The *itonalhua* inhabiting the underworld are said to slowly disappear after death.

An individual's *itonal* is in greatest danger when its owner does not 'have a good heart,' *kipia ahmo cualli yollotzin,* or is not 'living well,' *ahmo cualli nehnenmi.* If an individual is living well by the precepts of the ancestors, in harmony with the traditions of the village, only a very powerful witch can cause him or her harm by taking the *itonal* to the underworld. For an individual with aberrant or confused behavior, the *itonal* can be easily taken either by a witch or by one of the supernaturals of the underworld. An individual who is not living well is in constant danger of losing his or her *itonal*.

The 'evil winds,' *ahmo cualli ehecat,* can also displace an *itonal*. A displaced *itonal* may be lost on the surface of the earth or in the underworld. There are some rare cases of an *itonal* visiting the sky, but these are not common. In order to treat a client suffering from 'soul loss' or 'magical fright,' *nemouhtil,* a curer must not only locate the lost aspect of the soul but also ascertain the reason for the *itonal's* loss. This is done through dreams. The practitioner's *itonal* travels in dreams to search for a client's infirmity.

The practitioner dreams to diagnose the causes of a client's illness and return him or her to health by restoring the soul to its proper equilibrium. In dreams, the *itonal* wanders the earth, the sky, and the underworld. The practitioner, armed with a particularly sophisticated knowledge of the form and shape of the underworld as well as the ways of the ancestors, searches for the cause of his or her client's problem. In most cases of nonorganic illness, it is the displacement of the *itonal* that is responsible for the client's condition.

Nagual: *Folk and Native Concepts*

The *inagual* is a very difficult concept to work with, not due to its complexity in the world of curing, but rather due to the vast literature on the concept in Mesoamerican anthropology (Brinton 1894; Foster 1944; Villa Rojas 1963; Aguirre Beltran 1983) and the vast differences in folk beliefs concerning the nature of the *nagual*. It is intimately entwined with witchcraft, nativistic movements, and curing. And it is vastly misunderstood.

There is in fact no single name for the third entity that makes up the human soul. Signorini and Lupo (1989: 55) chose *ecahuil,* shadow, which is part of the basis for this aspect of the soul but is inadequate in light of the importance of this aspect of the soul in dreams, curing, and witchcraft. Arriving at an actual name for this third aspect of the soul is probably arbitrary, for like the *itonal* it embodies a multitude of concepts that are rather loosely held together even in the opinion of practitioners. There was considerable debate with both Rubia and Inocente over this term, and they often did not use it in a coherent manner, especially Inocente, often confusing it with folk concepts of witchcraft with which he was quite familiar.[10]

As a name for this entity, I prefer *nonagual,* but it is not just the individual's animal alter ego; it is the complex of qualities that animate the darker side of life in the Sierras. It is intimately involved with both witch-craft and curing, and it is essential in dreaming, for *nonagual* is the only entity that can deal directly with the lords of the underworld. Practition-ers acquire a number of dark ferocious beasts as their familiars to aid them in their dreamtime journeys in the underworld. These are intimately asso-ciated in practice with poisonings, murders, and witchcraft.

Nonagual represents the savage or uncivilized aspects of a personality, the darker and more dangerous side of life. Here I must take care to point out that this is not some strange type of *Star Wars* theology, but that by the darker side of life in the Sierras I specifically mean those activities associated with witchcraft, night, cold, uncivilized or savage behavior, murder, and death.

It is, as McKeever Furst (1995: 143–73) and López Austin (1980: 256) have pointed out, the stench of death and the dark glow of things at night that is associated with *nonagual*. It is the smell of a savage animal, the smell of the cave, the stench of death and one's own animal alter ego. The alter ego is the other side of a personality that is embodied in the animal alter ego; it is the practitioner's familiar, assistant, transformer. *Nonagual* shares all of these qualities with the soul of its owner and is thus far more than a simple animal alter ego. The nature of an individual's animal alter ego is said to have considerable influence on the individual's personality.

The reason for preferring *inagual* to *ecahuil* for this entity is its intimate involvement in the practitioner's dreamtime journeys in the underworld. Curers and witches use this aspect of the soul to travel throughout the underworld and to transform themselves into a series of beings to protect themselves. The *inagual* is the aspect of the soul that is seen in the under-world and that must be used in dreamtime travels. The *inagual* can com-municate with the lords of the underworld and can be transformed into various beings there. The *itonal* may travel undetected in the underworld, but it is through the *inagual* that the practitioner directly confronts the underworld.

The curer, *tepahtini,* and the witch, *nagualli,* are potentially the same individual, as Signorini and Lupo (1989: 100) recognize. The curer treats illness of the spirit, whereas the witch seeks to cause illnesses or to have them caused by the supernaturals of the underworld. The adept practitioner in San Martín will not only know his or her own animal alter ego, but over the years will have found a vast array of other animals and inhabitants of the underworld that he or she can become in dreams using this aspect of the soul. For this reason *inagual* is the preferred term for this aspect of the soul, for the *inagual* shares not only the *tonal* of the individual but all of these aspects of the darker side of the soul as well. The term *inagual* also correctly implies that this is the cooler, darker, and potentially more dangerous aspect of the human soul that is kept by the lord of the animals in the underworld.

In dreams, many individuals claim to have seen or traveled as their animal alter egos, yet such individuals in San Martín will never say what their own *nonagual* might be. It is a common topic of gossip to speculate on the nature of one's *inagual*. Common *inagualhua* are dogs, pigs, doves, crows, rats, and mice. No one will dare reveal the nature of his or her individual *nonagual*. To do so would be an invitation to witchcraft. The name of one's *nonagual* is a closely guarded secret, for a witch with that knowledge could simply insert the name in his or her supplications (Lupo 1995: 89) and cause the individual great harm. Some people do know of the nature of their own *nonagual* through their own dreams, and others will consult specialist practitioners with whom they are either related or to whom they have ties of ritual kinship to find out about their *nonagual*. It could be fatal to consult a potential witch in such matters.

Every practitioner must seek out his or her own *nonagual* and learn the geography of the underworld in dreams. As the practitioner progresses, he or she will find other animals and underworld beings that are amenable to becoming the individual's alter ego, or *nonagual*. Once a practitioner has dreamed of such a new ally, he or she can, with proper ritual, acquire the new nonagual and take on that animal form in the underworld of the ancestors.

NAGUALISM

In dreams, all practitioners are the transforming witches, *nagualli* or *naguals*, prevalent throughout Mesoamerica. The single most perplexing difficulty with *nagualism* in Mesoamerica since the earliest studies is the diversity of the concept within a homogeneous framework. From the almost fantastic efforts of Brinton (1894) to interpret the phenomena as a secret society (which Aguirre Beltran [1983] showed was not that far off with respect to nativistic movements like those of Martin Ocelotl [Gruzinski 1989]), the notion has been closely associated with obscure, secret activities. Brinton's guess that there was a secret society behind such beliefs is backed up today in the way that such esoteric knowledge is passed from practitioner to practitioner.

The relation between this knowledge and witchcraft makes practitioners highly secretive about their actual practices. There are lineages (Grinberg-Zylberbaum 1987) of practitioners who must pass on their own secretive knowledge of both curing and witchcraft to their disciples. This secretive information, and these practices, in fact, were probably passed down as a corollary to curing practices for generations, yet none would acknowledge them, for to do so would immediately open one up to charges of witchcraft. Thus, the covert lineages of curers and witches, which could easily be seen as secret societies by the uninitiated, have been a relatively unknown part of Mesoamerican religious practice for generations.

Foster's (1944) study, while seminal in showing that nagualism revolved around a set of beliefs in the power of individuals to transform themselves into other forms, did not touch on the central point of the transformation of the soul. López Austin (1980: 244 and 416–42) pointed out the fundamental distinctions between nagualism and tonalism, where an aspect of the soul is projected into an entity as opposed to being shared with an entity. Alfredo López Austin (1980: 430) notes that these two concepts are often confused not only by academics but by indigenous peoples. Traditional practitioners, however, are quite clear in distinguishing them as shared and projected aspects of the soul.

The practitioners with whom I worked made the fundamental distinction between the bound form *nonagual,* 'my nagual,' and the noun *nagualli,* a 'transforming witch.' Both Rubia and Inocente vehemently denied having anything to do with witchcraft since the end of the War of the Witches in the late nineteen thirties, yet I found evidence of witchcraft on Inocente's altar several times and once even caught him on tape discussing the type of witchcraft that a client wanted done to her daughter's wayward husband (Knab 1995: 1–13).

Inocente and Rubia emphasized to me that the techniques of nagualism were essential to the curing practice but should never be discussed with the uninitiated for fear of witchcraft accusations. In the earliest stages of my training, I was queried mercilessly about my dreams, the animals therein, and what I saw or did in them. To satisfy my taskmasters, I had to look at my dreams with their Mesoamerican gaze, placing things and events into a context that they would understand. Once they had determined the nature of my fundamental animal alter ego, *nonagual,* the one with which I share *notonal* or 'my destiny,' each of them individually showed me their private collections of buzzard beaks, rat bones, deer hooves, claws, bones, and skins from the numerous animal naguals that they could become. One even pointed out that some of his collection came from "real killers." Inocente illustrated some particularly sinister techniques of poisoning, or attacking a victim, associated with particular animals, while denying that he would ever use such methods.

Each practitioner taught me his or her own technique of acquiring another *nonagual.* Both techniques require prayers and offerings at one's own altar followed by a lengthy period of observation of the animal of interest. The animal must then be captured and killed by hand, although Inocente admitted to shooting several of the animals he had taken. A piece of the carcass of the animal then had to be taken to the cave and thrown inside so that it was returned to the lord of the animals. The rest could be consumed while keeping but one small reminder of the animal.

Once one has acquired a new *nonagual,* it suffices to take out the bone or feather kept under one's own altar, or simply to remember that it was there, before beginning a dreamtime journey to the underworld. The larger and more ferocious one's *nonagual,* the more efficient one could be in cajoling the underworld lords and the better one was protected from witches, which are a constant danger.

IMBALANCES OF THE SOUL AND DISEASE

There are numerous ways that the human soul can be out of balance with its natural, social, or supernatural environment. It is on the basis of direct personal experience of *talocan* that specialized practitioners of the healing arts can, by manipulating aspects of the human soul, restore the balance and harmony between the natural and supernatural worlds.

Although not all curing depends exclusively on the *curandero's* knowledge of the underworld, it is an essential part of the practice. Determining how and when to intervene in the realm of the supernatural requires an intimate knowledge of the nature and structure of the human soul, as well as an intimate knowledge of the underworld. The psychological metaphor implied by the nature of many diseases of the soul is an integral part of their treatment and cure. These metaphors are of the same type widely employed in modern psychiatry and psychoanalysis, and they fulfill the same function.

At the first meeting with a potential client, a native practitioner must determine the type of illness in order to recommend the proper treatment. An illness can be organic, caused by an infection or wound or some other type of physical ailment. If the ailment is determined to be physical, a combination of herbal teas and sweat baths is usually recommended, or the client is sent to see medical personnel at a local clinic.

If it is determined that the infirmity is not of an organic nature, there are several ways that the soul may be out of balance with the world. It may be any of several widely recognized infirmities of the soul. There is a distinct manner of treatment for each type of infirmity of the soul, and each type of illness implies some distinctive type of imbalance or dislocation of the soul. The loss of the *itonal* due to 'magical fright,' witchcraft, or its theft by supernaturals of the underworld can result in death. The inhabitation of the body or *iyollo* by an 'evil wind,' an 'evil glance,' or some type of malevolent object introduced into the body by a witch can also bring about an end to life on the surface of the earth. Damage or injury to an individual's animal alter ego, the *inagual,* as well as its capture or imprisonment in the underworld, will also result in death.

Unintentional imbalances of the soul can be the result of falling on a path or in a stream, for example, such as in most cases of 'magical fright,' or it can be due to an 'evil wind' that inhabits the body or any of a range of other causes that result in a fundamental imbalance or dislocation of the soul. Intentional imbalances of the soul can be caused by witchcraft, envy, lack of attention to proper traditional duties and ways of life, and other actions that provoke malevolent retribution either by the inhabitants of the surface of the earth or the underworld. Such cases imply that an individual is not living well, *ahmo cualli nehnemi,* or according to the precepts of the ancestors.

In all these cases, the native practitioner must rely on one primary technique to diagnose and treat the malady: dreams. Prayers (Lupo 1995: 103–107) are said at the household altar invoking the saints and the lords of the underworld; offerings may be made of flowers, cane liquor, and candles; the client may be pulsed, sucked upon, or massaged, yet it is through dreams that the practitioners can travel to the underworld of their ancestors, *talocan,* to find an adequate diagnosis. Dreams are the primary mechanism for knowing the unknowable: the world of the ancestors, *talocan.*

Not all dreams take place in the underworld of the ancestors. They may occur on the earth or in the sky. It is only the trained practitioner who can recognize where he or she is in the world of dreams. He or she is the only one with the burden or charge of bringing these dreams back to the world of waking consciousness. Dreams escape. They are difficult to 'carry' out of the world of sleep (Tedlock 1987).

Dreams are important in San Martín for many reasons. They may be portents of the future. They may be journeys to the underworld. They may represent the conflicts of everyday life and potential volition or resolution. They may be journeys to the celestial paradise, unattainable for man, where the saints, virgins, and Jesucristo reside in the world of holy light, *nexti.* Dreams may have a multiplicity of meanings and interpretations, all of which are important in the everyday life of villagers.

Dreams may represent journeys either in time or in space. There is great interest in dreams that may harbor portents of the future. Dreams may imply past or future events, but that is always difficult to determine, for the world of dreams is dark and indeterminate, carefully guarding its knowledge from the waking world.

Practitioners who have learned to dream for a purpose, who have learned to send their *itonal* or *inagual* in search of lost souls, take great care before dreaming. They make offerings and pray for the return of their soul, yet they are prepared at every minute never to return to the land of the living. Trained practitioners know the world of dreams and in a way fear it. It is fraught with danger for the soul and always holds the possibility of death.

CHAPTER TWO

DREAMS AND DREAMING

Journeys of the Soul

THE KNOWLEDGE OF DREAMS is as much a part of everyday life in San Martín as is the experience of the waking world. Everyone dreams, and everyone is interested in dreams. As in many cultures, dreams are everyday events that influence human action in the waking world (Tedlock 1987).

Most people in San Martín look to dreams as portents of the future or corrections of the past, but there are also dreams that are the province of trained traditional practitioners of the healing arts. Trained specialists have an elaborate system of knowledge about the supernatural and effectively use that knowledge to treat their clients. They have specific ways of recounting, analyzing, interpreting, and using dreams. In the process of recruitment and training, practitioners must learn the proper prayers, the offerings, as well as the form and structure of the underworld of the ancestors, *talocan,* in order to recount their dreams in an effective manner.

That practice will be discussed in subsequent chapters. Here we'll explore the role of dreams in everyday life—what makes them such an important part of the culture and in what contexts they are used.

Dreams in general are by no means the exclusive province of trained practitioners. Prayers (Lupo 1995) and narratives (Knab 1983a) that people have heard, or overheard, tell of the worlds of the earth and sky that can be seen in dreams, but these are not the worlds frequented by most dreamers. In contrast with trained practitioners' complex, formal system of knowledge, most villagers have only a vague general idea of the world of dreams, with few specific notions of its form, content, or structure, yet dreams play a significant part in their lives.

EVERYDAY DREAMS

Dreamtime is neither past nor future, and dream events may take place either in the earth, on the earth, or in the sky. Dreams are not always clear, and some individuals are reputed to have the ability to "see more clearly" than others in dreams. Nor are dreams always remembered. Some individuals "bear their dreams on their backs" to the waking world better than others. Some also recount their dreams better than others.

Children will often be asked to recount their dreams in the morning, on the path or in the kitchen while making tortillas. Then parents will recount their dreams. There is no fixed way to recount dreams, though there are certain narrative conventions.

No matter when dreams are recounted, there is usually a rather casual discussion of what they mean. Most anyone can hazard a guess as to the nature of a dream, and unlike in other parts of Mesoamerica (Bruce 1975; Laughlin 1976), there are few fixed interpretations. In San Martín there is no cookbook for interpreting dreams, although there are some motifs that are usually given the same interpretation over and over. Even rather standard interpretations, though, can and do change according to situation.

People say that events that occur in dreamtime are not clearly seen. They are vague, dark, and nebulous. They are unlike the events of the waking world, as only part of the individual perceives them. Only an individual's *itonal* travels in dreamtime, and its travels are, for most people, seen as random wanderings. What makes dreams important is the fact that an individual's *itonal* can wander through both time and space. The events seen in dreams may represent the past, not necessarily as it was, but rather as it could have been, and they may be signs of future events that could occur. The events of dreams are never taken as necessarily true, for they are not seen clearly. The individual's *itonal* can also travel in dreams to places that cannot be seen in this world, to the supernatural world of the ancestors, *talocan,* and to the heavens of the saints, *ilhuicac.*

The usual dreamer has no notion as to where or when dream events occur. Specialists, however, have clear and concise notions of dream events and are trained in recalling and recounting the events of dreams. They are the exception in the village of San Martín, and their dreams can have great influence on their clients. Still, the events of everyday dreams recounted in San Martín can and do influence social life there.

A dream can be the portent of future disaster, telling the dreamer to avoid certain activities. A dream can reveal the past perpetrator of harm, telling the dreamer to avoid a certain individual. A dream can conceal revelations or prophecies of the supernaturals of both the sky and the underworld, which can change the actions of individuals. A dream can reveal the true nature of events or be a complete falsehood. For this reason, the events of dreams are widely discussed, interpreted, and recounted.

Dreams are not solely mechanisms of divination, although they can hold the portent of future events and divine contacts with the world of the supernatural. In fact it is rather rare that dreams directly reflect future events, and when they do it is generally in an obscure way. A dream that is felt to have accurately foretold a future event is recounted again and again. It is a rare gem that sparkles from the mounds of dreams that have no clear meaning.

Most villagers will tell of one or two events in their lives that have been foretold by dreams: the attainment of a post in the civil or religious hierarchy, a marriage, a death in the family, or some similarly significant event. They will not, however, recall the many cases where the events of dreams were proven incorrect.

Many activities in daily life are said to be foretold or even dictated by dreams, from the selection of dancers and officials for the annual festival of the town's patron saint to the guilt or innocence of a potential witch. The events of such dreams, however, reflect as much the consensus of villagers as they do the recalled events of the dream. There is a willingness to frame such decisions in mystical events such as dreams. From the time a dream is first recounted until it loses interest and is discarded from memory, it may be transformed and reinterpreted by each individual who is aware of it, constantly changing the opinion, even of the dreamer, as to its implications.

Recounting a dream is cause for speculation and interpretation. It must be discussed, its meaning interpreted and speculated upon, for it to become a part of everyday life. Some dreams are never recounted, yet they form part of an individual's rational composition of the realities of the events of everyday life. These are harbored as secrets and may never be told. Other dreams are the common currency of everyday conversation. They may be told by children and discussed by parents, or they may be topics of family conversation while harvesting coffee. Yet other dreams may hold the portent of who is selected, and who is not, for important positions in the town.

In a society where the events of dreams have a direct effect on everyday life, their interpretation becomes a significant event. Once a dream has been recounted, either in casual conversation or more formally, it is then open to interpretation and speculation. The events recounted in dreams are generally familiar from everyday life in the village: getting water, clearing land, planting corn, harvesting coffee, etc. Fantastic and fierce animals may be encountered in dreams, including the *yolcameh,* the *tequani,* and various venomous serpents. These may be *nagualmeh* of witches trying to capture an individual's *itonal* or they may be apparitions of underworld lords castigating an individual for some transgression against the traditions of the ancestors. Such apparitions in dreams usually send individuals to seek the advice of a trained practitioner, as the dreams could have the serious implication of witchcraft, impending infirmity, and even death if not heeded.

Individuals, both living and dead, are seen in dreams, but they are rarely mentioned in dream narratives. There are several reasons for this curious situation. First, seeing an individual in a dream implies that it is the individual's *itonal* that is seen and not the individual. A disembodied *itonal* is highly susceptible to attack, mischief, or ill will, which could do an individual harm. Children are often told not to mention people seen in dreams. Not only is doing so impolite, but it is potentially dangerous. If the individual should fall ill, there is the possibility of the dreamer being accused. Second, seeing the living and the dead in dreams is a fearsome event that leaves ones own *notonal* vulnerable. It is therefore a matter that is best kept private. It is frightening and potentially dangerous, especially if one sees a notorious witch. Seeing the dead, especially, implies that they may be seeking one's own *notonal,* and it is best not to tell others about this, lest they presume one is as good as dead.

Privately many people will admit to seeing both the living and dead in dreams, but they almost never weave them into dream narratives. Most

individuals in dream narratives go politely unrecognized and are simply
identified as "this man" or "that woman." Whom such individuals might
be is always a matter of considerable speculation, and the dreamer generally politely refuses to confirm or deny their identity.

The everyday type of dream interpretation carried on by villagers
centers on several points that are quite different from those that are significant in dreams that cure. For most villagers, the questions center on,
first, whether the dream is a true event or only a possible event. Secondly, is it a portent of the future or could it be something that has happened in the past? Third, what are its implications in everyday life? I.e.,
should the dream really be considered in planning events?

Speculation on the nature and meaning of dreams is common conversation, and nearly everyone in town is willing to offer an opinion
about a dream. Speculation about dreams represents a constant and ongoing dialectic of thesis and antithesis of interpretation (Voloshinov/Bakhtin
1973), which may end with an interpretation that is part of everyday
action or may become uninteresting and be forgotten until a more
important and clearer dream event comes along. A good example of this
process is the way I was told of a friend's son's death in the Sierra:

> Martín was an old friend of mine. When I returned to the Sierra
> several years ago, I saw him and of course asked about the rest of
> his family. His son Ramos would have been eighteen by then. Not
> seeing him, I supposed that he had been married and was living
> elsewhere or was off working, perhaps in some insidious urban
> slum as so many villagers did.
>
> This was not the case, my friend informed me.
>
> Death, he said, had come and taken Ramos away.
>
> Ramos had never been a strong young man but had not been
> sickly either. When I had last seen him, his teeth were too big for
> his mouth and he was just beginning to grow up. He was always
> helpful and constantly watched me when I lived with the family.
> He was curious and caught on quickly to things.
>
> When I asked Martín what had happened, I expected him to
> tell me of some kind of tragic accident, but this was not the case.
>
> "Well, it happened in a dream," Martín began in a narrative
> style I knew well from the many tales he had told me.

It was his *tonal,*
that's right his *tonal* that left him.
It wandered off.
It went away.

Well you know that he did not hold it well.
He didn't keep that *tonal* of his with him very well.
When he was very small, when he was just a baby
it didn't stay there [pointing to the top of his forehead].
We bound it in.[1]
We bound him up and kept him warm.
Well, it didn't stay there though.
Marta[2] saw him in dreams
she saw the baby there near the water
she saw him there in the holy earth
she saw the little one, the baby there.
We knew death would come.
We thought he would visit us soon
but no not until a year ago
that's right nearly a year ago Ramos went with him.

Well the boy never kept it properly.
He never really held on to that *tonal* of his.
He would dream
he would dream all the time and
Woooffff!
offff,   off it would go!
off it would go!
Woofff! It was another magical fright.
It was another fright that got him.
He was always dreaming in the *milpa*
in the *cafetal*
in the garden
when we were hunting.
He never paid any attention.
He never looked for it.
He let it dream off.

Well he had a lot of *sustos,* a lot of frights.
Your old friend the witch tried to find that *tonal* of his
María tried to find it, and she did once in a while
but not often.
Marta knew.
She saw it   his *tonal.*
It was in her dream. It was there to see.
His mother saw it there.
His mother knew he would go.
She knew it all right
since he was a little one,   a baby.
One night it came.
One night death consumed the boy's heart, took it with him.
He had the *tonal* and took him off.
Woosh!
GONE!
DEAD!
He had Ramos.

Martín explained his son's death in his own way, not in terms of disease, but in terms of the boy's soul and dreams. This was a perfectly plausible and logical explanation in a world where dreams are real.

Villagers hold only a vague knowledge of the underworld; thus such dreams are revelations of the mystical world of tradition that they only partially understand. Villagers' knowledge of this world is far from complete, whereas the practitioner is considered a master of this tradition. Native practitioners are particularly interested in identifying where dream events occur in the world of dreams. This is their particular specialty and they will generally tell a client more about their surroundings in dreams than the events. This is because individuals in dreams are rarely discussed and because each location is perceived to have a specific implication as to the auspiciousness of events in the underworld. The method that these practitioners use involves an elaborate system of knowledge of the underworld of the ancestors, *talocan.*

The World of Dreams in Narrative

In contrast to the elaborate system of knowledge of the underworld of practitioners, what is known to most villagers of *talocan* in the world of dreams comes from the prayers and tales that are told on rainy afternoons where people gather—in *cafetales* and at people's homes. These may be the kinds of tales that anyone can tell, or they may be the province of well-known narrators whose ranks are dwindling.[3]

Generally information about the underworld is tangential in tale telling. It is a place for action, or it is a mystical setting for the fantastic to occur. It may portend cataclysmic and fantastic events, but it is rarely the central theme or location of a narrative, even a dream narrative. The vague understanding that most villagers have about the underworld is not a systematic form of knowledge. Even dream narratives told casually by parents to children, or by children to their elders, are not framed in the elaborate context of a journey to the underworld the way traditional healers construct dreamtales for clients.

In narrative, mention is made of the underworld of the ancestors in various regions of the Sierras (Taggart 1983; Reyes 1976). We know that beliefs still remain about the underworld, yet the complexity of these beliefs is only hinted at in most narratives. Alone, narrative does not encapsulate traditional beliefs or people's own knowledge of the underworld of tradition. It consists of mechanisms for elaboration of those beliefs. Narratives alone will never provide a clear picture of traditional beliefs. In village life, everyday dream narratives and dreamtales told by professional healers combine to form the basic outline of beliefs concerning the holy earth, but they alone are not the whole picture of the complex and coherent system articulated by practitioners.

In traditional narratives, mention of the underworld is not uncommon. It may occur in almost any of the narrative genre. The *tahtol tepitzin,* 'little words,' are the kinds of tales told almost anywhere under almost any circumstances (Knab 1983a: 129–42). They are the unmarked category of narrative that can crop up in conversation at the general store or while having lunch in the *cafetales.* Even in the simplest tales, though, there can be mention of the underworld or of its inhabitants, such as a tale of what has happened to a drunk who was discovered dead along the path to town (Knab 1983a: 230–34):

Well maybe he wasn't dead all day
but it was night when they found him.
It was those   those others   those who are not our brothers.
Those are the ones.
Those are the ones that got him.
They got that drunk
as sooooon as it was dark.
THOSE relatives of his shouldn't have stayed at Don Pablo's so long
because that's when those others got him.
I know it!

The "others" referred to here are the mischievous supernaturals of the underworld who captured the poor drunk's loosely held soul and took it with them to the world of the ancestors. The moral of the story is that the drunk's relatives shouldn't have stayed so late at Don Pablo's general store drinking. If they hadn't stayed so long, they would have found the drunk alive and taken him home where it was safe.

As a place for fantastic action in the *tahtol tepitzin,* Francisco Ortigosa Tello's tale of how the toad women became the servants and grinders of the underworld lords is an extensive example (Knab 1983a: 239–77). In the first section of the tale, which takes place in a mythic time, the toads become what they are today in a sort of Pandora's box tale. They are then taken in by a pair of nearly blind underworld lords who live in the cave and made to grind for them, an arduous task, on the *metate,* a traditional Mesoamerican grinding stone. The mischievous toad women loosed the winds kept inside the cave by the elderly twins. The winds blew some of the darkness of mythic times away, and the lords—in order to protect their domain from the light of the sky—had to shut the cave, leaving some toads inside and some out.

They (the underworld lords) were angry.
They were furious.
They wanted to shut that door
but they couldn't.
They couldn't shut it.
The winds kept it open.
They (the winds) were

blowing away the darkness.
They (the underworld lords) had to return to their hole
to their house.
They had to flee the light.
His (the sun/Jesucristo) light
His light had come to the earth.
They needed to shut the door.
All of their things would be blown out
blown away.
They pulled they pushed   they hit the rocks.
The mouth of the cave was shut.
Their door was shut
There were some toads inside.
There were some toads outside.
The toads that were outside were the ones
the ones that brought us light
that brought us the red and the black of the earth.

The red and the black is a standard Mesoamerican metaphor for knowledge, but Francisco had no idea of its meaning. For him it was simply part of the story. Practitioners though were well aware of its meaning. In this extensive and mythic tale, Francisco was able to elaborate on traditional beliefs using the underworld and mythic time as a setting for the action.

The *tahtol melauh,* or 'true words,' which have a formulaic termination asserting their veracity, make far greater mention of the underworld. These are the types of tales generally told for children that emphasize the moral nature of tradition. Dreamtales are sometimes told in this way to emphasize their moral weight as tradition in curing contexts. The underworld and its inhabitants, as guardians of traditions and castigators of transgressors of those traditions, are ubiquitous in this genre. In the tale of the *Mazacameh,* supernaturals of the underworld, and the drunk, this is quite evident (Knab 1983a: 315).

This little drunk is just arriving home.
the drunk comes to his house
and thiiis——this Mazacameh
gets him on
on the road.

Three of those
THREE OF THEM.

Those Mazacameh   tell him,
"We're going over here now—mister
over here
over here is YOUR HOUSE."

The inhabitants of the underworld attempt to capture the drunk and take him to the cave, but he escapes, or so he thinks. Upon returning home, he finds that he has not in fact escaped retribution, nor has his family (Knab 1983a: 316).

The Mazacameh
THEY GOT HER.

because they came as evil winds.

"You have brought them
YOU'VE BROUGHT THE EVIL WINDS
THOSE WINDS HAVE FOLLOWED YOU!"
said the
woman.
"You've brought them from the cave."

Then the Mazacameh
THEY GOT HIM.
THEY—GOT—HIM.

They entered this drunk
these Mazacameh
these little things
these *duendes.*

This is true.
IT IS CERTAIN.
IT IS FOR SURE
THAT IT IS TRUE.

Throughout the *tahtol melauh,* or 'true tales,' narrators weave together themes of tradition, moral values, and retribution with themes of the underworld and its inhabitants, emphasizing the moral fabric of the community and traditions.

The more extensive narrative genres such as the *huey tahtol* and the *huecauhcayot* make mention of the underworld and its inhabitants, but not with the same moral impact as the *tahtol melauh*. These epic genres are basically origin tales. In the case of the *huey tahtol,* two major figures from Spanish folklore, Juan Oso and Blanca Flor, become cultural heroes, establishing the worlds of men and women as they exist today. The *huecauhcayot* are a series of loosely connected tales recounting the origins of all things of this world.

In the *huey tahtol* there are such themes as when Juan Oso meets the keeper of the animals and, as part of an Oedipus-like series of connected narratives, when Juan finds his mother is a witch and sends her to *talocan.* Juan Oso encounters supernaturals of the underworld in the tales of the *alpixque,* or water keepers, the *tepeyolomeh,* the people of the hill hearts, and many other beings from *talocan* in the process of bringing the world to its present state. In the Blanca Flor tales, there are such themes as when the ill Blanca Flor sends her prince to *talocan* to find the old woman who brought her up to cure her and when the same old woman demands that Blanca Flor remain with her in the cave. These narratives provide general information about the role of the underworld of the ancestors in everyday life, but more as background than as a central theme.

As origin tales, the narratives of the *hueycauhcayot* genre begin with the origins of worms and things that crawl in the earth, progressing to snakes, deer, and people in one version that emphasizes the creation of all things from the earth. In other versions, they emphasize the origin of things as they are now. Again, knowledge of the underworld is tangential to the narratives themselves.

DREAMTALES

Dream narratives fit all the general criteria for tale telling in town. They usually fit within the *tahtol tepitzin* or *tahtol melauh* genres and can be told anytime or anyplace. They conform in content, context, and format to the general narratives that are a part of everyday life in San Martín (Knab 1983a). Dreamtales[4] are different in that they are not told outside the context of specific curings, and they generally fit the criteria of the *tahtol tepitzin* or *tahtol melau* narrative genres.

Accounts of practitioners' dreams told in the context of a ritual curing are different from everyday dream narratives. The content is limited
to the curer's narrative of a particular dream event, performed in the context of curing his or her client. The discussion and interpretation of the
dream event, which is central to the process of curing, may and often does
interrupt and interfere with the actual narrative. A practitioner often cannot finish recounting an entire dream due to the constant speculation and
discussion of the meaning of the dream for the client. This discussion is
highly valued.

In order to emphasize the veracity of a particular dream and give it the
moral weight of certitude as a parable for discussion, a practitioner will
often use the formulaic termination of the *tahtol melauh* narrative genre.
This is done especially when there are events in the dreamtale that the
practitioner feels the client and his or her family must consider fully. In
such cases, the practitioner—upon completing the dreamtale—will return
to particular themes, asking participants directly if they remember this
or that type of event in real life and what it could imply.

The practitioner seeks to elucidate the events of everyday life by
means of speculation on the nature and meaning of the dream event and
must therefore ask specific questions and seek particular explanations. The
practitioner, too, is uncertain as to the meaning of a particular dream
event and is seeking an understanding of it through dialogue (Tedlock
1995: 284). The practitioner adapts the dreamtime experience to the context of the client, and though he or she may have an idea as to the meaning of a particular dream for a client, it is through dialogue that a proper
interpretation is determined.

Narratives in San Martín are not singular events that are performed in
isolation. The narrative itself is a dialogue of constant interaction with the
audience for whom the tale is told, the metaphoric roots of the tale. Don
Inocente scolded me after my attempt to tell a tale as follows:

No, NO, no.
You do not speak your words.
You know the words but you do not speak them.
You do not say them for the roots
for me, for Lucio, for Don Tomás.
You say them like your *grabadora*[5] says my words.
You say my words too!

You know the words, your words, you can say them!
Why then do you not say them?
When you tell it, when you recount it
you say your words, you place your roots
here [pointing at Lucio and Don Tomás]!
Your words come from the root of your tale.
The seed sprouts and the roots come out first.
You speak to them. You speak from them.
Perhaps we are not good roots, then it withers and dies.
Perhaps you have no roots here, then you cannot tell the tale.
The seed does not sprout without the roots.
The thing becomes green with good roots.
The thing withers if you forget its roots.
It dies.

The narrator here was admonishing me for not having the proper inter-action with the audience in telling a tale. Telling a tale is an act like a metaphoric plant rooted in the interaction with the audience, with whom the narrator carries on a constant verbal and nonverbal dialogue.

Tale telling is constantly punctuated by audience interaction, which influences the form of a narrative. The formulaic audience response is *queman,* yes, with which the audience agrees with the narrator's tale and encourages him or her to expand on a particular theme. More extensive audience commentaries are found, but they are not nearly so common in ordinary narratives as they are in dreamtales. This type of commentary is typical of dreamtales used for curing in which the dialogue is actually the central feature of the event. The dialogue is in fact what makes the dream meaningful for the curer and client.

Making the Dream Meaningful

The curer bears a dream for the client from the vague and obscure world of tradition. He or she tailors it, alters and adapts the experience in the vague and obscure world of the ancestors to the client's situation and per-ceived problems. The curer "carries the dream into the light." The dream itself has no meaning. The meaning emerges through dialogue (Mannheim and Tedlock 1995: 14). Interpretation is arrived at through dialogue.

It is the interpretive dialogue that actually gives the dream meaning (Mannheim and Tedlock 1995: 15). They adapt it to their perceived view of the events of everyday life in the waking world. The dreamtale is a text that is embroidered through multiple possible interpretations (Tedlock and Tedlock 1985). A single dreamtale can have many possible interpretations. Although the way in which a dreamtale is fashioned for a particular client may represent the practitioner's hypotheses about the nature of a client's problems, it has no meaning without dialogue (Bakhtin 1986: 159–72).

The practitioner seeks to learn of the events of everyday life that may affect the balance of the soul of the client in the waking world. Since dreams are such a common topic for speculation, dreamtales recounted in the process of curing are an especially fertile field for conjecture as to the client's problems, both in the everyday world and in the supernatural world.

Each time a practitioner dreams for a client, he or she adapts the dreamtale to the understanding of the client and the client's particular problem. The practitioner relies on any information that can be gleaned from the client; the client's friends, relatives, and siblings; and local gossip in the process of searching the world of tradition for the cause of a particular problem. Restoring the balance of the soul in everyday life is in a sense a metaphor for bringing the individual's life back into accordance with the traditional norms.

In a world where dreams are real, they are a potent tool for interpretation. They are also potent explanations of the events of everyday life. Working dreams of trained practitioners and the dreamtales that are formulated out of such dream events are specific, concise, intentional attempts to maintain harmony in the waking world by manipulating the unconscious world of the supernatural.

Working in Dreams

The underworld of tradition and the ancestors, *talocan*, can be visited by many villagers in their dreamtime travels, yet it is the trained practitioner who frequents this realm and who is often consulted about it. According to practitioners, villagers may visit the underworld with some regularity, but they do not recognize it as such. In fact, uninitiated villagers often look with fear on the prospect of frequenting the underworld of their ancestors. It is seen as a place of danger, darkness, and death, a world better left to the professional experts in the supernatural and their counterparts, witches.

There are few specialists in the world of dreams. A poor town cannot support a massive, highly specialized priesthood of dreamers. Two factors, however, have further diminished the number of practitioners in the region. The first is that the inroads of modern medicine have taken many clients from traditional healers. Many of the diseases that traditional practitioners treat, however, are not amenable to the miraculous cures of modern medicine, and Western practitioners are slowly realizing this. Today traditional specialists will often work hand in hand with Western practitioners. Unfortunately, much damage has already been done to the traditional client base.

The other factor that significantly reduced the ranks of traditional practitioners in the region was the infamous War of the Witches of the twenties and thirties, a rural agricultural conflict fought covertly with a type of witchcraft that consists of some very sophisticated techniques of poisoning victims, attacking them in ways that are all but undetectable and transmitting rare tropical diseases (Knab 1995). Practitioners are capable of both healing and harming an individual. In the aftermath of the War of the Witches, there have been few new recruits to the traditional healing arts who are willing to take the mantle from native practitioners who well may have been witches too. Today there is an almost universal denial that witchcraft even exists in the village.

The elderly practitioners in the village who have learned the ways of the world of their ancestors have trained few new followers in San Martín. Don Inocente trained one woman from another village (Almieda 1987: 112), and Doña Rubia trained no one from the village (Islas and Sanchez 1987: 147). The other two practitioners in town have likewise, to my knowledge, trained only one individual from the village in their tradition. Even Don Inocente's son, himself a healer, has refused to take on the full burden of his father's tradition, fearing its association with witchcraft.

It is essential for practitioners to train someone in the ways of their ancestors so that their own souls may have repose in the underworld of the ancestors (Almieda 1987). Although practitioners have not always managed to do so in San Martín, the tradition is not dying. As indicated in the prologue, there are still many followers of the *cualli ohti* or good path.

Initiates into the traditions of the ancestors can be recruited in several ways. First, individuals who have suffered severe cases of *susto*, or soul loss, or those who have been bewitched, may have to take on some of the burden of the tradition in order to alleviate their own maladies. This is the way many previous practitioners were recruited.

Today, such individuals rarely take on the entire burden of the tradition, but they learn enough of the meaning of dreams to become relatively adept curers, even though they don't actually practice. Such individuals have specific obligations to the world of the ancestors for the remainder of their lives. They must make constant offerings to the lords of the earth. They must regularly pray before their family altars. Their dreams are generally deemed more significant than those of other individuals and are more thoroughly discussed by all. Today, such individuals understand more about the tradition of the ancestors than most other villagers, but they are by no means expert practitioners. They generally have not learned to search out a lost soul (*itonal*) in dreams or to transform their own soul (*nonagual*) in the underworld.

The second way in which practitioners are recruited is by request. When a curer consistently dreams of a particular individual, he or she may approach that person with a request that they learn to pray and dream. This was a common method of recruitment in the period of the War of the Witches, and practitioners generally recruited only members of their own families or lineages: allies. The request was more than a mere invitation, for an individual could suffer great physical harm by not embracing the tradition. It was an offer one could not sensibly refuse. New recruits were considered at great risk until they mastered the prayers and techniques of sending their souls into the underworld in dreams and transforming them, which is also an essential technique of witchcraft.

The third type of recruit to the practice was not chosen by practitioners, but rather by the lords of the earth themselves. These were individuals who had survived lightning strikes, snake bites, near drownings, and in one case battle wounds.[6] Such individuals sought out practitioners to show them the tradition. They were called by the earth lords.

All new recruits had to learn three fundamental techniques for dealing with the world of the ancestors. First, they had to learn the prayers and techniques of making offerings. Prayers are in effect offerings for the earth. Second, they had to learn to dream and to understand their dreams as journeys to the underworld of the ancestors. Third, they had to learn the nature of their own animal alter ego and acquire additional alter egos their *nonagual* could inhabit in the world of dreams. This aspect of the tradition is intimately related to witchcraft.

The process of learning to dream is gradual. One cannot be told how to dream. It is more the interpretation of dreams that one learns, and gradually the ability to direct the dream through a series of techniques from autosuggestion to sympathetic magic. Learning to dream is learning the world of the ancestors—its form and structure and the techniques of dealing with it in everyday life. Learning the geography of the underworld and the prayers and techniques of curing provides a framework for viewing dreams that is grounded in tradition.

It is essential to learning to pray and make proper offerings to the lords of the earth before learning the 'proper' ways of dreaming. The prayers are repeated and repeated until the long litanies become part of one's own consciousness.

The offerings can be rather substantial for subsistence farmers and do represent a significant commitment to the training process. The rituals connected to making the offerings are quite exhausting, requiring the initiate to spend considerable time in caves, along cold mountain streams and waterfalls, or on unprotected mountaintops.

Like the prayers, the rituals teach the initiate the form and structure of the world of the ancestors in an indirect way. Symbolically the offerings also represent the knowledge of the underworld that the initiate must internalize to learn about the world of dreams.

Specific offerings are made to the lords of the four sides and the center of *talocan*. Flowers representing the underworld are placed in the center of the offerings. The lords of the underworld are offered nourishment, tortillas, beans, and water. They are promised ritual sustenance and vows of lifelong maintenance, such as the regular burning of candles and incense. Offerings of tobacco and *aguardiente,* a potent local cane alcohol, are made for the spirits of the powers of darkness too.

In prayer, the powers of the night are admonished and threatened; they are made well aware that all offerings are reciprocal. The initiate must bargain with the powers of the underworld to show him or her the realm of night. The initiate must offer his or her own heart, *noyollo,* as a part of the commitment to the world of the ancestors and traditions. It is only after nights of prayer and offering that the initiate's soul, *itonal,* is recognized and able to travel to the underworld of the ancestors.

The investment in time, effort, offerings, and rituals that is required of the initiate before beginning to learn to dream is phenomenal. Prayers and rituals from the initial offerings to the earth in the cave are constant and repeated ad nauseam. In the early stages of training, the initiate is drilled constantly and allowed little sleep. The practitioners will recount dreamtime journey after journey. The initiate is then expected to recount each detail of his or her own dreams. Those not conforming to the general pattern of dreamtales are urged to work harder to bear the dreams on their back into the waking world.

It is at this point that one realizes that the dream itself is in a way irrelevant, for the experience of dreams can be described in many ways. With the constant repetition of prayers, rituals, and the interpretation of dreams by practitioners, one begins to discover in one's own experiences the threads of similarity. The world of the ancestors and dreams are congruous with those places mentioned in prayer, those journeys constantly repeated in recounting dreams, and those symbolically reiterated in ritual. Slowly one begins to find in one's own dreams the same things that are part of the constantly repeated and reiterated world of the ancestors. The more that one knows of the underworld of the ancestors, the easier it is to fit one's own experience into that world and interpret it in the same terms.

The form and content of the underworld is the result of a dialectic of tradition with experience. Each new practitioner must find in his or her dreams the fixed points of the underworld of the ancestors and traditions. This implies that the initiate must also learn the nature of each of the four sides of the underworld and the supernatural beings who may inhabit them. This is done through a combination of experience and instruction.

Trained practitioners analyze the dreams of the initiate, sifting them for any trace of an experience that might be analogous to their own knowledge of the nature of the underworld, sometimes asking specifically leading questions like, "Did it appear watery?" "Did you see this clearly?" or "Was there smoke or fog?" Practitioners will carefully explain the characteristics of each section of the world of darkness, what is there and why it is there. In this way the initiate is instructed in the proper form and structure, the nuances of the world of dreams that he or she should be seeing so that it will be recognized when it is actually encountered in a dream.

In this process of instruction, the initiate begins to understand the obscure and fluid nature that is attributed to the underworld, and that it is in a very real way a means of talking about the events of this world. It is a way of speculating on the basis of the supernatural about what is correct and proper according to tradition. Dreams in this way become a vehicle for speculation about the nature of experience and relations in the waking world.

The initiate's search for the four sides and the center of the underworld is in this sense a metaphor for his or her grounding, through instruction, in the conceptual principles that govern Mesoamerican cosmovision. In the process of finding the center and four sides of *talocan,* the initiate learns not only the fixed geography of the underworld but the vast array of flexible places of indeterminate location that become an essential part of the metalanguage of dreams. The metalanguage is fundamental in forging a dreamtale that is meaningful for both curer and client. This metalanguage of dreams is a basic tool in curing that a practitioner uses to speculate on the nature of experience in the everyday world based on the world of tradition and the ancestors.

Understanding Dreams

Understanding dreams involves extensive instruction in the form and nature of the underworld and its traditions. It also involves understanding how dreams are viewed as vague, obscure experiences that must be borne into the reality of the waking world. A dream experience may be told in a multiplicity of different ways. When telling a dreamtale, dream experiences past and present may merge in order to speculate, or project, on a notion about a particular event or experience.

Some fundamental points about understanding how practitioners view dreamtime experience and dream events that they recount are essential. First, the world of dreams is dark and obscure. Thus the experience is never completely clear or transparent. Second, since dream-world events are generally viewed as timeless, various dreamtime experiences can be merged in the dreamtale. Even dreamtime events that are relatively clear are often merged with others, or reinterpreted. Since dreamtime events are generally recounted for a client to make a particular point, there are some things that must remain secret. The client would not understand them or would be needlessly frightened by them. Such things include the contact with the souls of people living or dead; the techniques of trans-

forming the soul, *nonagual,* into different animals; specific demands or pro-
nouncements of the lords of the underworld; and the threats of witches.
In the telling of a dreamtale, the dream is specifically modified for the
context of its telling and those it is told for.

The events of dreams that practitioners recount for their clients are
generally those that take place in the multitudinous places of indeterminate location in *talocan.* They are connected by identifying the places in
which such events could take place in everyday life on the earth and generally are associated with those activities on the earth, *talticpac.* In this way
they are speculations on the relationship of real events in light of basic
points of cosmovision. There is a strong moral component to dreamtales,
illustrating traditional values and ways of doing things. In effect, they illustrate the dialectic of tradition and morality (Bakhtin 1968).

A practitioner will generally indicate how the underworld of the
ancestors is entered either before beginning the actual tale or as an initial part of the dreamtale. The entryway is often arbitrarily chosen as a
place a client would recognize. Entryways can be cave mouths, deep pools,
streams, sinkholes, hot springs, rock crevices, mountaintops, deep canyons,
etc. Entry into the underworld can also be said to occur from falling
down or from being hit by falling objects or lightning. In one unusual
dreamtale, one of the practitioners was snatched by an evil wind, *ahmo
cualli ehecat.* In another, the practitioner was snatched by a magical bird,
a *cuixi,* which happened to be her own *nonagual.*

Practitioners often say that entryways are not recognized clearly. It is
thus preferable to choose one that a client would know or recognize.
When a curer dreams for a client, the dream must be a network of events
that the client and his or her family can understand and relate to. The
way that a practitioner recounts a dream for another practitioner and the
way he or she recounts it for a client may sound like two completely different tales.

In the nature of dreams there are certain types of displacement that are
relatively common (Herdt 1987: 58, 67). These are described in ways that
fit with the curer's expectations of the client and his or her situation. The
events of a dream from the first entry into the underworld, *talocan,* are
strung together in a seemingly random manner. The curer goes from place
to place in the underworld, sometimes walking, sometimes traveling in a
stream, and sometimes flying on a bird or as a bird. The order of events in
the dream are often reordered by the practitioners to make them more

understandable. This is what is meant by the common metaphor for creating a dream narrative: "bearing the dream on one's back." The practitioner must take the dream experience and transform it into the expected form in the way that he or she feels will be acceptable to the client.

The events that occur in dreams, such as washing, gathering coffee, harvesting corn, and hunting various animals, are generally tailored to a client's normal everyday activities. Often a curer will not have a single specific vivid dream experience and the entire narrative will be composed of these vague events wandering through the various places of indeterminate location in the underworld searching for a client's lost soul. These are sometimes the most successful dreams for the client and his or her family, who will project on them significant aspects of their own everyday life and indirectly tell the practitioner the nature of perceived problems.

Even when there is a single specific vivid event in a dream that would be worthy of recounting, the practitioner may delete it from the dreamtale if it would be too difficult for the client to understand. These events may also be too personal to recount. One of the practitioners would regularly tell me of conversations with her ancestors and lords of the underworld, which she considered privy information and concealed within her dreamtales. She would transform direct conversations with supernaturals to overheard conversations regularly. She would also clearly state that she could transform herself into various animals in the underworld but only on rare occasions would recount such events for clients.

The way in which dreamtime travels in the underworld of the ancestors are recounted depends on two factors: the expectations of the curer and client and the interpretations of the curer and the client. The practitioner is not a charlatan simply inventing fantastic tales for the client but is rather working both for the client and the traditions of the ancestors. Developing a dreamtale is not a simple matter of recounting vivid events.

After one particularly long session, Doña Rubia explained the nature of dreams in a way that was far better than I could. She switched into Spanish for her explanation, peppered with Nahuat terms for clarity.

> You know when you take up the dream, you take it out into the light from *talocan,* the darkness. The dream is there in the holy earth, but it is your burden, your duty to carry, *titamemiz,* you carry

it on your shoulders you put on the tump line there in the darkness in *talocan,* and then you have to carry it out into the holy light, you have to take it from the fog and the darkness on your back. You take it up there in the darkness, in *talocan,* and you have the dream there in the darkness, but you have to put it on, you have to take up the burden. *Nehnemi ipan in talocan,* it lives there in the holy earth, and you take it, but it wants to return, it wants to go back down, but we need it here on the earth, *in talticpac, in nexti,* in the light. You have to take the damned thing out! We need to know if they have it, or they have seen the soul, *itonal,* of Fulano. We need Fulano. His mother will cry, his family will cry, they will not have as much coffee, they will not have someone to help with the corn fields. Those damned things want to keep it there in the night, in the darkness, in *talocan.*

It is not important that you see Fulano, but you must take up the dream you have, to give your account of it. It is your burden. You can't just speak, just recount, you must carry it to them you must make it clear, *titanexti, queman,* yes, Maybe they will know, maybe they will tell you something, that is why you must present them your burden, your load, your pack. The thing is your burden and it is your gift to them, they pay for it. You recount it well. You take them your tale. That is your burden, your duty.

In curing, dreams are recounted a day or so after offerings have been made and prayers have been said for the aid of the supernaturals of both the sky and the underworld. This alone gives the client and his or her family certain expectations as to the content of the narrative. The images and implications extracted from overheard devoutly mumbled prayers and the offerings that reiterate humankind's continuing obligations of sustenance and maintenance are clues. The ritual structures the expectations for the dream.

The dreamtale necessarily recounts a journey to various points in the world of the ancestors, and it may or may not include dramatic episodes of tension and danger, especially of the curer's escape, which can make a prosaic sojourn in *talocan* a dangerous battle. The dreamtale may involve deceit and trickery, or even epic battles, to locate a client's lost soul, *itonal* or *inagual.* Yet its essential feature is that it must be a narrative that a client and his or her family can relate to and interpret in terms of their own everyday lives.

Each time the curer dreams, it is an attempt to determine the nature of the client's imbalance in the everyday world. The dreams are, so to speak, sent to different parts of the underworld. The curer does this by sympathetic rituals on his or her own family altar. If it is suspected that the soul has been lost in a particular place, then the curer will leave offerings at an equivalent place on the surface of the earth, or the curer may send the client or the client's family out to leave such offerings. In this way, as in many of the prescribed rituals associated with this type of curing, clients and their families, even their friends and acquaintances, become active participants in the search for a cure of the client's maladies.

Dreaming for a Client

The curer is a specialist who must make the world of the ancestors seen in dreams intelligible to his or her client. This is done by transforming the dreams into a metalanguage that uses dreams to discuss the world of everyday life in terms of the traditions and values of the world of the ancestors, *talocan*. Two examples of a particularly problematic dream will illustrate this point. The first example is the dream as explained to me in the process of learning to interpret dreams, and the second is the same dream as explained to a woman of about eighteen years, Chela, who was suffering from magical fright, *susto, nemouhtil.*

The dream was explained to me as follows:

> It was in the hills along a stream where I was walking and the stream began to take me. It carried me in the water down to the bottom and into the sixth great river and to the third falls where I could escape. I walked along the edge of the river and came to a wide open plain where there was a good road, one of the royal highways, the sixth, I think. They were there all right, those *ahmotocnihuan,* those who are not our brothers, but they didn't see me there I was just a dog along the path and there were many of them there as dogs, maybe some of them were witches. They were talking there on the path and some of them were going to a vigil. They would get good food there they said. You know those things

eat the dead, they hold the wake before some poor soul dies, not like we do after. What they're waiting for is lunch.

Well, they said that it was in the third hill heart of the underworld, where they were going to. That's a long way on the sixth highway you have to go to the center and find the third highway and go to the *tonalan* side to find the third *tepeyolot* of *talocan*.

So, I ran off the path and into the forest and the brush. There I found my dove. I went with her. I flew up and over to the third hill heart. It was darker in there and my dove wouldn't go, not inside. You could hear them though. You could hear them waiting, that was where they kept the vigil. They were singing and praying. They were dancing and talking. They were playing the drum and the flute. Someone was going to die, sure enough some poor soul would die.

There was a little hole there near the entry where my brother the rat hid. I went up to him and told him to come out.

"Take me in there!" I told him.

"No, they'd eat me there," he said, "surely those things they'd see me there and they'd eat me too. They're hungry; why, they're waiting for their lunch down there."

"Take me there! I have good corn for your brothers in the sun, and I smoked my tobacco anyway they won't get me there. Take me!"

Well, I went in there, into the *tepeyolot*. They were dancing. There were *tocatines* there and there were *quetzales*[7] there. It was dark and there was smoke there with the drum and the flute but I could see nothing. They were waiting for lunch there. I went further to the third cave pool and I saw some of them going to where the vigil was kept. I had to see whose vigil it was. Maybe that was where they kept Chela. I saw my uncle, the *nagualli,* down there but he didn't see me. He didn't cry out. I looked for others maybe Antonio, Chela's father, who died last year, but I saw no one.

Then they got me!

One of them exclaimed, "There's tobacco. I smell tobacco, ayeee!"

And I ran out of there. I was lucky; they couldn't see me in the dark, but they sure could smell my tobacco in there. A rat is small and I ran fast to the opening.

There was my dove and I jumped to her. We flew up and out to the light. That was it. It's over. I didn't see the poor soul they're going to eat.

The same dream was explained to the client, Chela, later that day in the following manner:

I was at a well to draw water and I went to the bottom of the well. From the bottom of the well I came to the great river and the falls that is there in *talocan.*

There I got out of the water and I walked along to a flat area like the one where you go to wash. And there was a *camino real* there, like at the *ahuetzic* [8] where you go. I could see the *ahmotocnihuan,* those others there.

They were going off to a fiesta; they were dressed in white and had on their finest headdresses. [9] They were all talking and I could hear them there talking about the fiesta. You know what that means when those others have a fiesta; It means someone is going to die! They were going to one of the enchanted places, maybe a cave, maybe a hill heart, maybe a hilltop, maybe a great deep pool.

I followed them there along the way and I flew ahead of them on their path. They were all on their way to a wake there in *talocan.* They were all of someone's ancestors. They were all going to welcome someone. They all come out to celebrate when someone is going to die. They have their wakes before someone dies there in *talocan.* They do that when they've already got someone or a part of someone, her *tonal* or her *nagual,* because shortly they'll get her *yollo,* her flesh. When a witch gets someone, he gives them many things, he makes them some offerings, he pays them off, and they can begin the preparations for a fiesta.

I arrived at a great pool there where they were all waiting. There were dancers there and flutes and drums. There was a fiesta all right. I crept up where they wouldn't see me near the pool where they kept the poor *tonal.* They kept it there, they kept watch over it so it wouldn't get away. Maybe a witch paid them, or maybe they were just hungry. Maybe it was someone without a good heart, someone who did not live well, or maybe it was just someone who had fallen or been knocked about or been lost. Well they had some-one there, and they were keeping 'em.

I went closer to see who was there, whose vigil was being kept there in *talocan*. Then one of them cried out.

"There is one with meat here! I smell it! There is one who is of flesh yet. There is food here!"

They knew I was there, and they were going to get me there. They would eat me there!

Wooosh! I ran off into the forest, through the brambles over rough stones and then there was a bird there.

"Quickly," I said, "take me out there. Take me up to the light!" And it did. We flew out into the light.

In the first example, the curer was emphasizing the numerical indicators of indeterminate places, which she had been trying rather unsuccess-fully to teach me to use for both interpretation and navigation in the underworld. She explained the entry into the underworld to me in terms that a man was expected to understand, as men often hunt along the streams in the hills and forests of the region. The gender adaptation of the tale was essential, and her purpose in telling me the dreamtale was clearly didactic.

The version for her client was necessarily different in that she used none of the numeral indicators and in no way mentioned her ability to transform herself in the underworld. She adapted the tale to a woman's point of view. Women rarely will walk the paths along streams except to do the wash, and then they prefer large open streams where others gather. They do often go to the wells alone to bring back water.

The curer offered the client's family several points to speculate upon. If the event was a fiesta and there were dancers, could the client's trans-gression have involved an indiscretion at a festival or could it have been on the way to a festival? Was it the client whose wake was being pre-pared? Was the client's problem due to something that happened in another village, perhaps at a festival? Was this due to an indiscretion on the part of the client or another of her female relatives?

The version for Chela's family contains a range of things that they could speculate were the cause of her soul loss, and this is what they did.

Everyone discussed the dream and many other matters well into the evening when Rubia left. The dream was inconclusive but highly productive.

Rubia had suspected that Chela had a lover or admirer from near San Andres who was probably disapproved of by the family. They confirmed that Chela and her mother often went that great distance with the wash. This seemed suspicious to Rubia, as she later commented, adding that perhaps it wasn't Chela but her mother who had a lover there. Her only request was that the family leave offerings at the pool near where the women did their wash for the poor lost soul that was kept in the underworld. She had suggested that perhaps the soul she saw was Chela, but no one seemed to agree with the idea. Perhaps there wasn't a lover involved, she further speculated, as no one objected to the offerings.

Another dream that will show the range of experience in the underworld is the dream Rubia had in the late twenties which she said was one of the factors that made her embrace the tradition of the ancestors. The dream so horrified her that she got little sleep thereafter. It was a repetitive dream that would not leave her. This convinced one of her relatives, another practitioner and one of the combatants in the War of the Witches, that she had to embrace the traditions of her ancestors or be consumed by the holy earth. Her mother and grandmother, as well as many of her maternal relations, had embraced the tradition, which they maintained had come from Totonac refugees, probably at the time of the French invasion (Islas and Sanchez 1987: 184). Rubia had little confidence in these traditions before this dream began to recur.

> Well, it always started out that I was at a well. Sometimes I was there for water with a big jug and sometimes there was wash to do there, but there was always the well there, and I reached into the well. It came up and it grabbed me there at the well and pulled me into the water.
>
> I went down and down into the darkness in the water and something held me and it took me it carried me there in the water further and further into the darkness. I was held. I was bound there in the darkness and rushing down in the water. I was dragged there over rough stones up and down and then I came to rest there in front of another well like the first one but I couldn't move and it

came out and grabbed me again with big black arms that took me in, and it was even darker and the water went faster there in that place.

I could hear it rushing all around and I came to rest at another well but the water was whirling there and it too took me in and down into the darkness around and around like a spindle whorl dancing up and down. I was beaten and bounced on the rocks and when I could see again I was there at another well with a great wind blowing the water all about. It was some kind of tempest or hurricane with sharp rain that stung and lightning. I wanted to wake up. I was frightened but I couldn't, and the tempest took me into the water again. I think the tempest was so great that there was water everywhere.

I came to rest again at another pool that was calm. The water was like a mirror. It was dark and I was bound. I couldn't move. I was sure I had drowned.

I could see something there in the water or on the water there were two great bright red eyes there in the darkness. There was a terrible smell and there was not a sound. Then there was a dripping. Each drop I heard clearly. Ploosh, ploosh, ploosh! It became like the drum they use to call the men to work at the church.

The water was turning red and it was boiling. And I could still see the two great eyes coming closer. It was steaming and boiling; there was fog, mist, and the eyes started to come out at me. Then I saw the teeth. Long sharp teeth all the same, not like a dog, or a *tequani*. All of them were the big teeth. They were snapping open and shut, making the water boil. The eyes came closer and closer and the smell was rotten. I was bound! I couldn't move! It was going to eat me! I could hear the chomp! Chomp!

Then I saw darkness and usually awakened cold and sweating. When I didn't awaken there was a woman there seated at an altar. She was all in white *naguas* with a great headdress and she was speaking, but I couldn't hear anything. She was huge, but she wasn't frightening. Sometimes there was a little man with her, perhaps a dwarf. I walked closer and closer to hear her but couldn't hear anything, and as I climbed the altar with steep steps the little man was waving his arm and getting very angry. He moved his mouth too,

but I heard nothing. Finally I came right in front of the great lady
and the dwarf began to push me, but I could hear her she said,

"*Xicaquiz! Xinohnotza!* Listen and recount this!"

I fell down the stairs of the altar and most of the time woke up
there.

The few times that I did not awaken I saw my father from far
away who said, "It is not good! It is not true!"

Rubia was afraid to tell her mother of the dreams, but she did go to a
maternal uncle with her problem. She was told that the earth would consume her and that she must embrace the tradition of the underworld. She
was of the opinion that the woman was a virgin at first, but her uncle
found that it appeared to be her grandmother whom she had never
seen. As for her father, she was told he was probably a witch and trying
to prevent her from taking on the tradition. She would surely die if she
didn't. This was at the time of the War of the Witches, and her father had
been on the opposing side in the conflict. I was never able to determine
if he simply abandoned her mother and his family or if he had died perhaps due to witchcraft. The family simply refused to speak of him. There
were many accounts however of how her mother had to raise the family
alone.

This dream, together with the two versions of the previous dream,
begins to indicate the range of dream experience of practitioners. Most
dreams are not as dramatic as the last one, and it should be noted that this
was a rare repetitive and personal dream that served as my only example
of how a curer was recruited. In general most dreams were more similar to the first two versions of one dream.

The practitioner's task is not an easy or simple one. It is a practical
method that seeks to balance tradition and everyday life in an ever-
changing context. Balancing tradition and change, the practitioner uses
dreamtales as a vehicle for projection. The act of curing is both concrete
and metaphoric. The practitioner is a master of the nebulous world of tradition, bringing together metaphors and meanings that function at many
levels within the social fabric (Tedlock and Tedlock 1985). The practitioner conjoins the world of darkness and tradition with the events of
everyday life, allowing villagers to project their notions of how everyday
life should be structured onto dreamtales of tradition.

In the process of learning to dream, recount dreams, and cure, prayers are the primary template for understanding the underworld of the ancestors. The long litanies of places in the underworld provide the initiate with the first notions of the geography of the underworld. Learning to understand dreams under the tutelage of a trained practitioner allows the initiate to "see" these places in dreams. The process of learning to dream is the process of learning not just the geography of the underworld, but its traditions, the proper ways of life, *cualli nehnemi*. 'Living well' maintains the precarious balance of the soul between earth and sky.

CHAPTER THREE

"I BESEECH THEE MOST HOLY EARTH"

Prayers for the Earth

PRAYERS AND INCANTATIONS are perhaps among the most culturally revealing of all rhetorical forms. Not only do they encase and preserve fossilized remains of past cultural epochs with archaic language, but like myth, they form the templates deep in the unconscious for the actions of everyday life. Prayer, like myth, is the prototype against which cultural concepts, symbols, metaphors, and meanings are compared. To understand systems of Mesoamerican thought in cultural terms, prayer is a fundamental epistemological tool.

Much of what is heard of a prayer, when properly said, is as vague and indeterminate as a dream.[1] The uninitiated may know a few prayers, usually short offertories, supplications, or benedictions for the old fire gods or the lords of the Most Holy Earth (Lupo 1995). Such prayers are often not even recognized as prayers; they are simply what is always said when the fire crackles, or "speaks," or when the earth lords are "paid."

These are not the elegant forms of supplication, cajolery, wheedling, and sometimes even admonition and threat that are used in the prayers of practitioners. Learning to pray and make offerings is an essential part of the training of any practitioner. It is part of the process of learning the form and structure of the world of the ancestors and learning how to deal directly with the supernaturals of that world. The prayers represent an essential part of the dialogue of earth and sky.

The practitioner is a master of dealing with the world of the supernatural. His or her prayers are one of the few manifestations of the knowledge a practitioner possesses of the supernatural. So, learning to pray in the most elegant and fervent manner is of great value for the practitioner. Though a client may not understand much of what is mumbled at the household altar in a curing ceremony, the fragments of a prayer that are understood are highly regarded as important remnants, remembrances, tokens of the relationship with the Most Holy Earth, *talocan*.

Life on the earth alternates between light and dark, danger and salvation, deprivation and grace, and in order to live on the earth, a balance must be struck between these two realms. This balance is one of the fundamental features of Mesoamerican relationships.

A curer seeking the cause of a malady of the soul must request the aid of both realms of the supernatural to be successful (Lupo 1995: 116). He or she must request, cajole, and play off the interests of the sky and the earth as in the following passage:

Axcan xinech maga![2]
Axcan xinech temactia   nehin conetzin!
Hualazque nochinin Arcángeles, serafines, querufines, ángeles milagrosos,
*   ejercitos de angeles.*
Xihualaz totemaquix ticatzine   San Miguel Arcángel!
ica mosanto espada
ica mosantisima cruz   banderada de oro.[3]

Xihualaz, xinechpalehuiz!
Xicon polihuizque, xicmo tamizque
ica motanextilo
ica mosantisima luz!
Tehuatzin tihualaz in mostoc
axcan ahmoniquitta mo fuerza motanextilo.

Nican in talocan
nicanin yohualichan

nimechtatauhtia   nen conetzin   nen espiritu.
Nican nimechaxcatili ica tantos oraciones
nican nimechtemaktia nofuerza notonal.
Cani yetoc nehin?
cani ancpiah toconetzin?
Pox ticonmacazque tehuatzin
tehuatzin nimitztatauti.

Now give him to me!
Now let me have   this child!
All of the Archangels will come, seraphim, cherubim, miraculous
     angels, armies of angels.
Our Savior   San Miguel Archangel will come
with his holy sword
with his holy cross   draped with gold.

Come! Help me!
Destroy him! Finish him off,
with your light
with your holiest light!
O, sir you will come in the morning's light
I no longer can see your holy light, your power.

Here in the *Talocan*
here in the house of darkness
I beseech you   this child   this spirit
here I offer you such prayers
here I let you have all my strength, my soul.
Where is this one?
Where is our child being kept?
Would you give him to me O, Sir
O, Sir I beg of you.

Balancing the interests of the supernatural against each other is essential
in prayer. The curer maintains relationships with the underworld much
as he or she maintains relationships with other villagers in San Martín.
The curer promises and threatens the lords of the underworld to get his
or her way, as in the above passage, always maintaining the essential balance between sky and earth, light and dark.

Prayers for the Lords of the Earth

In prayers demanding the aid of the lords of the underworld, the lords are addressed directly after seeking the aid of the sky and its holy "light" for protection. These prayers are legion, for in curing, planting, divination, dreaming, and witchcraft, for example, the aid of the underworld is essential (Lupo 1995). The supplicant seeks the aid of the entire underworld, beseeching, demanding, and threatening its inhabitants. The adept supplicant plays off the two realms of the supernatural, one against the other, in seeking aid. After requesting the aid and assistance of the sky, the saints and virgins, the adept supplicant may demand:

> *Xinech palehui!*
> *Tehuatzin, talocan tatoani*
> *tehuatzin, talocan tagat*
> *tehuatzin, talocan cihuat*
> *tehuatzin, taloc!*
> *Xi nechpalehui*
> *ipanin talocan*
> *ipanin moreino*
> *ipanin yohuayan!*
> *Xinechpalehui*
> *ipan in mictan*
> *ipan in eheca!*

> Help me!
> You Sir, Lord of *Talocan,*
> you Sir, *Talocan* Master,
> you Madame, *Talocan* Mistress
> you Sir, *Taloc!*
> Help me
> there in *Talocan*
> there in your domain
> there in darkness!
> Help me
> in the land of the dead
> in the land of the winds!

Taloc and *talocan* are the darkness, wind, and death, male and female, yet they are man's sustenance. As Aramoni (1990: 165) also points out, they make life on the earth possible:

> *Talocan tinotaxcal nantiani.*
> *talocan tinotaxcal tatiani.*
> *taloc   tinotaxcal nantiani.*
> *taloc   tinotaxcal tatiani.*

> *Talocan* you nourish us as a mother.
> *Talocan* you nourish us as a father.
> *Taloc*   you are our tortilla mother.
> *Taloc*   you are our tortilla father.

They are both male and female at the same time, source of life and place of death, father and mother. The very nature of both *taloc* and *talocan* is dualistic, and yet one must determine if they are the same. This is a crucial question for understanding the meaning of *taloc* and *talocan*.

The dualistic nature of both taloc and talocan are fundamental features of the ancient substrata that make up Mesoamerican cosmovision. Although this kind of dualistic relationship may seem contradictory in that sustenance and life spring forth from the underworld, a place of death, this is a fundamental feature of Mesoamerican religious thought.

Taloc *and* Talocan *in Prayer*

The way prayers are structured makes them dualistic in nature (Aramoni 1990: 161). The prayers touch on not only the relation of man to the supernatural, but the basic concepts of the soul and man's place in the world (Signorini and Lupo 1989; Lupo 1995; Knab, 1991).

Prayers are said to determine the location of a lost soul or object. They are said with offerings in thanks for the earth's bounty. They are said before dreaming. They are said for protection from witchcraft and much more (Lupo 1995).

Although most practitioners will readily discuss *talocan* and its nature, the word *taloc* is rarely heard outside the context of prayer, and discussions of *taloc* are always forced. *Taloc,* as the embodiment of *talocan,* is seldom recognized overtly. The prayers are for the most part formulaic, yet what they reveal about the nature and form especially of the underworld is manifested nowhere else in the culture. At times, prayers, couplets, triplets, quatrains, and larger verses elegantly address both *taloc* and *talocan*. This is almost the only instance where the term *taloc* is commonly used. Here it is obvious that *taloc* is the embodiment of *talocan*.

> *Tohueytatzin titaloc*
> *tohueynantzin ipan in talocan*
> *tohueytatzin ipan in talocan*
> *tohueynantzin titaloc.*
> *Xinechpalehui ipan in moreino*
> *xinechpalehui ipan in moyohuala!*
> *Xinechhuica nican in yohualan*
> *xinechhuica hueca in yohualan!*
> *Xicaquiz cualtzin!*
> *Niquitoa nen!*
> *niquitoa axcan!*
> *Tehuatzin   totatzin huan tonantzin, talocan.*
> *tehuatzin   taloc, tinechoncaqui.*

You are our great father *Taloc*
our great mother in *Talocan*
our great father in *Talocan*
you are our great mother *Taloc.*
Help me where you reign,
help me in your darkness!
Help me here in the night,
help me throughout in the night!
Hear this well!
Here I say it!
Now I say it!
You Sir, our father and our mother, *Talocan*
you Sir, *Taloc,* hear me.

TALOCAN: THE WORLD REFLECTED

Taloc is both mother and father, both male and female, and both the place and its embodiment, yet *talocan* is a place with many locations within it.[4] Note how the realm of *talocan* is defined in the following passage:

Cani yetoc?
ce monahui yohuayan?
Ahmo niquita oc mofuerza motanextilo
cox oc ce malo moconeuh quitemoac.

Tiquitac nohueytatzin taloc
axcan tehuatzin nohueynantzin canica tiquitaz.
Ximohualaz temohuecan ca ipan!
Cox yetoc mahtactionahui cuauhtameh
cox yetoc mahtactionahui tepemeh
cox yetoc mahtactionahui   tepeximeh
cox yetoc mahtactionahui   acacmeh
cox yetoc mahtactionahui   apitzacmeh
cox yetoc mahtactionahui hueyameh
cox yetoc mahtactionahui pozomeh
cox   yetoc mahtactionahui   tonalehecat
cox yetoc mahtactionahui   ahmocualliehecat
cox yetoc mahtactionahui   mixtimeh.
Tehuatzin taloc   tiyetoc mahtactionahui   cuauhtahmeh
tehuatzin taloc tiyetoc mahtactionahui tepemeh
tehuatzin taloc tiyetoc mahtactionahui   tepeximeh
tehuatzin taloc tiyetoc mahtactionahui   acacmeh
tehuatzin taloc   tiyetoc mahtactionahui   hueyameh
tehuatzin taloc tiyetoc mahtactionahui pozomeh
tehuatzin taloc   tiyetoc mahtactionahui   tonalehecameh
tehuatzin taloc tiyetoc mahtactionahui ahmocualliehecameh
tehuatzin taloc tiyetoc mahtactionahui   mixtimeh.
Xiquitaz   xicmatiz   AXCAN xiNECHitoaz!

Where is it?
Is it in one of your four places of night?
I no longer see the power of your light.
Could it have fallen with one of your evil children?

You see it my great father *taloc*
now my great mother where do you see it.
Come here with it!
Could it be among the fourteen forests
could it be among the fourteen hills

could it be among the fourteen   mounds
could it be among the fourteen   channels
could it be among the fourteen   ravines
could it be among the fourteen rivers
could it be among the fourteen wells
could it be among the fourteen   warm winds
could it be among your fourteen   evil winds
could it be among your fourteen   clouds.
You taloc are   the fourteen   forests
you taloc are the fourteen hills
you taloc are the fourteen   mounds
you taloc are the fourteen   channels
you taloc are the fourteen ravines
you taloc   are the fourteen   rivers
you taloc are the fourteen wells
you taloc   are the fourteen   warm winds
you taloc are the fourteen evil winds
you taloc are the fourteen   clouds.
You see it!   You know it!   Tell ME NOW!

In this passage, not only is the nature of the underworld defined, but so is the nature of its inhabitants (Knab 1991). All of them are aspects of *taloc* and *talocan*. The entire pantheon springs forth from *taloc* and *talocan*—the very notion of the underworld itself.

Taloc is the *taloc melauh*, or 'true *taloc*,' who resides in a cave in the conceptual center of the underworld (Knab 1991). *Taloc* is the *talocan cihuat* and the *talocan tagat*, the *señor taloc* and the *señora taloc* or *talocan*. *Taloc* is the *presidente talocan* and the officials of *talocan*. The *taloc melauh* is at once the lord and lady of the realm as well as all the officials of the realm. Although not commonly recognized as such, in fact all the supernaturals (Knab 1978) of the underworld are but aspects of the *taloc melauh*. The *taloques*, the *talocanca*, the *alpixque*, the *mazacameh*, the *kiyauhtiomeh*, etc., are all aspects of the *taloc melauh*. This is best demonstrated in the following passage where the practitioner is trying to flatter the lord of the underworld to obtain a favor:

Tehuatzin tohueytatzin tohueynantzin titaloc
tehuatzin talocantagat talocancihuat titaloc
tehuatzin talocan presidente, aguaciles, fiscales, nontaloc.

Namehuantzin talocanca   taloque   talocanca   taxcaltiani   nontaloc
namehuantzin mixtemeh   ejecameh kiyauhtiomeh nontaloc
namehuantzin ahuane   alpixque   achihuanimeh nontaloc
namehuantin tepehuane tepeyolomeh   tepemeh nontaloc.
Nechtapohpolhui miec
nimitztatauhtitia itech nehin yohualli
nican nimitztauhtili ica nehin moraciones
nican nimitzaxcatili.
Ica nehon nitatiani favor.

You our great father our great mother are *taloc.*
You lord of *talocan* lady of *talocan* are *taloc.*
You the president of *talocan*, executioners, wardens, are *taloc.*
You *talocanca,   taloques, talocanca   taxcaltiani*   are *taloc.*
You *mixtimeh,   ehecameh, kiyauhtiomeh* are *taloc*
you *ahuane,   alpixque,   achihuanimeh* are *taloc*
you *tepehuane tepeyolomeh,   tepemeh* are *taloc.*
Pardon me greatly
this night I will beg of you
with these prayers I beg you here
here I offer them to you.
I ask you this favor.

By telling the lord of the underworld that everything is in fact a part of
him, the supplicant hopes to flatter a favor out of the underworld.

The following is a version of the very simple prayer said by people
leaving offerings for the underworld at the mouth of the cave. First one
seeks protection from the sky and then one offers sustenance to the earth
in the form of bounty from the new harvest. Chicken and turkey hearts
as well as candles and copal are also common offerings at the cave, the
entrance to the underworld.

Dios totatzin
Dios totatzin
tinechpiaz, tinechpalehuiz
huan.[5]*//*

Tehuatzin talocan tagat, talocan tatoani, nochin oficiales de talocan
tehuatzin talocan cihuat, acihuat, miquicihuat,
nican nimitzmagaz nimitzaxcatiliz motacua   motapalol.

Xictacuaz tehuatzin
xicayiz tehuatzin!
Tehua ximotamacaz
tehua ximotequipanoaz!
Ahmo ximoamiccehui ica noconetzin!
ahmo xicmahcehua ica nosimil!
Nimitztequipanoaz, nimitztamaca
nimitztasocamati   tehuatzin
miec tasocamatic, tehuatzin.

God our father
god our father
protect me, help me!
and.//

You, Sir, lord of *talocan,* Speaker of *talocan,* all officials of *talocan*
you Ma'am, Mistress of *talocan,* Mistress of the waters, Mistress of
     death
here I will give you, I will offer to you, your food, your sustenance.
Eat Sir!
Drink Sir!
Nourish yourself!
Sustain yourself!
So that you should not slack your thirst with my child!
so that you should not consume my fields!
I give you sustenance, I give you nourishment
I give you thanks   Sir
many thanks, Sir.

In this sense, man both maintains and sustains his own beliefs in the
underworld. And that underworld is what represents man's beliefs in the
unknown, for in prayers there is a leap of faith that constitutes an affir-
mation of the unknown. The seemingly contradictory dualism is resolved.[6]
Practitioners see no conflict between *talocan* as a place of death and the
sustenance of man, or between *taloc* as mother and father. They also see
no difference between the 'true *taloc*' and all of the supernaturals of the
underworld. They are all aspects of the world of the ancestors living and
doing what they would on the surface of the earth.

Talocan: *A Journey to the Unknown*

In prayers, curers seek to travel to realms that cannot be known. In order to find a lost soul or divine the location of a lost animal, a curer will dream and in that dream will travel to the world of his or her ancestors: *talocan*. Before dreaming, however, one must pray both to the sky and the underworld for aid and guidance, as in the following passage:

In ompa in talocan
xinechuicaz xinechpalehuiz!
Nictemoaz ompa in moreino
nictemoaz ompa in talocan.
Cani yetoc?
Cani huitztoc?
Cox huitztoc?
Cox icatoc?
Cani yetoc nehin espiritu?
cani mocahuac iyolo?
Xinechuicaz ompa in moreino
xinechuicaz ompa in talocan
xinechuicaz ompa in yohualichan!
Nicnequitaz nejin conetzin
nicnequi nejin espiritu.
Xinechuicaz ipan majtactionahui tepejmej!
Xinechuicaz ipan mahtactionahui tepeyolomeh!
Xinechuicaz ipan mahtactionahui cuauhtimeh!
Xinechuicaz ipan mahtactionahui tepeximeh!
Xinechuicaz ipan mahtactionahui   hueyameh!
Xinechuicaz ipan mahtactionahui   axalmeh!
Xinechuicaz ipan mahtactionahui cuali ohtimeh!
Xinechuicaz ipan mahtactionahui tacotonameh!
Nictemoaz   nehin espirito
nictemoaz iyolo
nictemoaz nehin moconetzin!
Cani yetoc?
Huan, yehuan quiquitzquitoque?
Yehuan quimajpachotoque.

Mah quimahcahuacan.
Xinechpalehuiz notatzin, nonantzin
xinechuicaz in ompa in talocan!

Take me throughout the underworld!
Help me!
I shall search for it throughout your domain
throughout the underworld I shall search for it.
Where is it?
Where has it fallen,
Has it gone?
Is it standing there?
Where is this spirit?
Where has this soul fallen?
Take me throughout your domain,
take me throughout the underworld,
take me throughout the house of darkness!
This child, I want to see it
this spirit, I need it.
Take me to the fourteen hills!
Take me to the fourteen hill hearts!
Take me to the fourteen forests!
Take me to the fourteen mountainsides!
Take me to the fourteen   rivers!
Take me to the fourteen   sandy rivers!
Take me to the fourteen good paths!
Take me to the fourteen trails!
I will search for   this soul
I will search for his heart
I will search for this your child!
Where is it?
And, where are they holding it?
They are keeping it.
They must leave it go.
Help me my father, my mother
take me throughout the underworld!

Travel in the underworld takes place in dreams deep in the unconscious mind, yet for one trained, as Rubia was, in the ways of dreaming
and interpreting dreams, this experience is every bit as real as those of the
waking world (Knab 1995). Dreams constitute a direct and personal experience of the underworld. They are a link with the unconscious world of
ancestors and traditions, yet few except those trained in the prayers and
the ways of *talocan* can appreciate their deep significance.

The prayers constitute one of the primary road maps that define the
geography of the underworld (Knab 1991), belief in the unknown and
unconscious world of ancestors and traditions. They are a manifestation of
man's relationship with the unknown world of ancestors and traditions
that give that world form and meaning. This is a direct personal experience of the underworld of the ancestors and their traditions.

When a curer seeks to travel to the underworld, prayer constitutes
the primary plea for aid in dealing with the world of the unknown and
unconscious so that it may be made clear and conscious. Early in a prayer,
a curer will seek the aid of both the saints and sky and the underworld
lords to search, for example, for a lost soul (Lupo 1995: 116–18) or the
cause of a disease.

Tehuatzin xinechpalehuiz!
Tehuatzin xinechuicaz!
Temaquixtiquetine Jesucristo
axcan tehuatzin   ipanin   Santo gloria tireinaroa.
Tehuatzin todios nochinin talticpac,
xinechpalehuiz!
Xinechcuicaz!
Xinechteochihuaz!
Tehuatzin Señor Miguel   Arcángel,
Príncipe, arcángel, coronel, general
general   de nochinin arcángeles
timohualaz titemoaz in santo gloria.
Xinechmagaz monex   mosantisima luz!
timohualaz titemoaz in santo gloria
xihualaz xihualpanquisaz nican itech moluz tanecic!
xiyecon nican!

Nican mo santisimacruz   banderada de oro
nican mo santoespada
xinechtatohuiz ica mo santo gloria!
xinechpalehuiz ica moneci mosantisima gracia!
Nehon icatoixnamiqui, ica ahmotocnihuan.

Tehuatzin talocan señor xinechpalehui!
Tehuatzin talocan cihuat xinechpalehuiz!

Noseñor nogeneral hualaz queman temoaz.

Cani yetoc nehin espiritu?
nicruegaroa nictatauhtia nehin iyolo.
Mah cahuacan nen conetzin,
mah cahuacan
mah uiqui.
Mahcahuacan nican
mahuico nican
Diosnuestro   salvador en santo gloria quinequi
nictatauhtia nen conetzin.
Anamehuatzin señores talocan
xiconmacazque!
Xinechmacazque!
Axcan xiconmaga!
Nen moconetzin moespiritu!

You, O sir, help me!
You, O sir, take me!
Our savior Jesucristo,
now Sir, you   are in   your domain of holy light.
Sir, our god throughout this earth,
help me!
Take me!
Make me holy!
You sir Archangel   Michael
Prince, Archangel, *Coronel, General*
General   of all the Archangels
come down in your holy glory.
Give me your light   your most holy light

you will come you will descend in holy glory.
Return! Arise with the light of dawn!
Be always with us here!
Here with your holy cross   and its golden banner
here with your holy sword
defend me with your holy glory
help me with your light with your most holy grace.
Those are your enemies those are not our brothers.

You Sir, lord of the underworld help me!
You Madame, mistress of the underworld help me!

My lord, my general come! Yes, come down!

Where is this spirit?
I plead, I beg for this his heart
O, leave this child
leave him
let him come
let him leave
let him come.
Our lord   our savior in holy glory wants him.
I ask you this child
You sirs lords of the underworld
surrender this child.
Give it to me!
Now surrender
this your child your spirit!

This is a powerful plea. First of all, the very plea itself is balanced between a request and a threat. It pits the powers of the earth against those of the sky. Secondly, it seeks to derive the unknown of the underworld from the known world by direct personal experience of that world.

> *Xinechmaquitztia!*
> *Xinechtatohuia!*
> *Xinechualaz, xinechuicaz, xinechtemoaz in santo gloria*
> *itech moneci in mostoc*
> *itech mosantisima luz!*

San Juan Lucero de la mañana
xihualaz nican!
San Miguel Arcángel
itech miec Arcángeles
milliones de angeles
xihualaz nican!
Santiago Caballero
xihualaz ica mo caballo!
Xihualaz ica mo espada!
Xihualaz ica morelampago ica ce tepetanilot milagroso!
Xinechtzacuilican ica nemoneci!
Xinechquitzquican ica namoangeles serafines!
Xinechmahpachocan ica namosanta luz
ica namotatiochihuaz!
Xinechhualaz xinechpalehuiz nican
ipan in tepemeh
ipan in tepeyolomej
ipan in cuauhtimeh
ipan in hueyameh
ipan in ixtahuameh llanos
ipan in pueblos
ipan in cuidades!
Cani yetoc? Cani moahi nehin conetzin?
Cox yehuan nehin ahmotocnihuan nehin kiotiome, nehin achihuanimeh
    quipiah?
Xa yehuan quipixtoque?
Nicnequi xicmaga!

Cox itech mahtiotanahui cuevas …[7]

Ma cahua nen toconetzin señor taloc.
Ma cahua nen señora taloc.
Ma cahua nen presidentes talocan.
Ma cahua nen fiscales talocan.
Ma cahua nen aguaciles talocan.
Ma cahua nen topiles talocan.
Ma cahua nen tenanches talocan.
Ma cahua nen jueces talocan.

Xicualazque nican tosalvador Jesucristo
San Juan, San Miguel Arcángel
Santiago Caballero.

Save me!
Defend me!
Come to me, take me, descend in your holy glory
with your light in the morning
with your most holy light!
Saint John Morning Star, first light of the morning
come here!
Saint Michael Archangel
with all your Archangels
millions of angels
come here!
Saint James Cavalier
come with your   horse!
Come with your   sword!
Come with your lightning, one of your miraculous lightning bolts!
Protect me with your light!
Hold me with your angels seraphims!
Keep me with your holy light,
with your blessing!
Come to me! Help me here,
in the hills
in the hill hearts
in the forests
at the rivers
on the plains
in the towns
in the cities!
Where is it? Where is this your child?
Could he be with those who are not our brothers, could a light-
     ning bolt, a water maker have him?
Could they be keeping him?
I want him! Give him to me!

Could it be that he is among the fourteen caves. . .

O, that you should free him lord *taloc*.
O, that you should free him lady *taloc*.
O, that you should free him presidents of *talocan*.
O, that you should free him wardens of *talocan*.
O, that you should free him executioners of *talocan*.
O, that you should free him deputies of *talocan*.
O, that you should free him ward women of *talocan*.
O, that you should free him judges of *talocan*.

Come here, Our lord Jesucristo,
Saint John, Saint Michael Archangel
Saint James Cavalier!

Talocan as a part of a sacred geography provides a mirror image of the real world in which man lives. But as we can see in these passages, the curer is seeking to bring some of that unknown and unconscious knowledge to bear on the problems of the real world of his or her clients.

Taloc and *talocan* constitute the ontological basis for such relationships in the real world, but only to the degree that they provide an ethno-epistemological method for deriving the known from the unknown. The real significance of *taloc* and *talocan* for native specialists is as a repository for the unconscious traditions that are the basis of everyday life in the real world. Concepts, metaphors, and meanings manifested in direct personal experience in the underworld are based on these principles.

The curer attempts to solve the client's problems by cajoling, beseeching, and otherwise convincing the lords of the underworld to get his or her way. Examine the following passage.[8]

Axcan xinechmaga
axcan xinech temactia   nehin conetzin!
Hualazque nochinin Arcángeles, serafines, querufines, ángeles milagrosos,
   ejercitos de ángeles.
Xihualaz totemaquix ticatzine   San Miguel Arcángel
ica mosanto espada
ica mosantisima cruz   banderada de oro!

Xihualaz, xinechpalehuiz!
Xicon polihuizque, xicmo tamizque
ica motanextilo
ica mosantisima luz!

Tehuatzin tihualaz in mostoc
axcan ahmoniquitta mo fuerza motanextilo.

Nican in talocan
nicanin yohualichan
nimitzhtatauhtia   nen conetzin   nen espiritu.
Nican nimitzaxcatili ica tantos oraciones
nican nimitztemaktia nofuerza notonal.
Cani yetoc nehin?
Cani ancpiaj toconetzin?
Pox ticonmacazque tehuatzin?
Tehuatzin nimitztatauti.
Cox huetztoc
cox icatoc.
Campa nictemoa?
Campa quipia
Campa quinenequi?
Cuicacan cani quitemoa?
Cuicacan cani tahtani?
Porque ahmo te nitatautoc.
Nican tamelhua
nicuelita nimotequipanoaz
nicuelita nipaquiz
nicuelita ninehnemiz.
Nimitztatautia icon tantos oraciones
nitatani icon tanto amoracion
timotekipanoaz, timonejnemitia
nimitztatautia.
Tehuatzin xinechpalehuiz!
Ma ompa yecan
ma quitemoazque
ma quinamiquizque
ma techcuicazque.
Xitechcuicacan nen!
Axcan nimitztatautia
xiconmagaz!

Hualazque nochin in arcángeles
nechmaquixtican in mostoc

nechmaquixtican ica motanextilo
xinechcuicacan in mostoc!
Ma niquittaz motanextilo.
Yehuan quiquitzquitoque.
Yehuan quimapachotoque.
Ma nen hualatiaz
ma quimajcahuacan
ma mitzhualatiaz
ma mitzcahuacan.
Quitatautia totemaquixticatzin Jesu Cristo
quitatautia San Miguel Arcángel.
San Juan Crecencia de dios
San Juan de la Luz
San Juan Lucero de la Mañana
José Maria Trinidad
Don Juan Manuel Antonio Marqués
Don Juan Manuel Martín Ocelo
Don Manuel Antonio Francisco Hernandez
Don Martín Antonio Francisco Abad
Santiago Caballero
General milagroso de la luz
Xinechcahuacan in mostoc!
Ma niquittaz mosantisima luz.

Tasocamatic
miek tasocamatic
amahuitzotzin nitasocamati.
Ica todo nofuerza
niquitoa.

Miec tasocamatic tosalvador.

Miec tasocamatic tehuatzin.

Now give him to me,
now let me have this child!
All of the Archangels will come, seraphims, cherubims, miraculous
    angels, armies of angels!
Our Savior   Saint Michael Archangel will come

with his holy sword
with his holy cross   draped with gold!

Come! Help me!
Destroy him! Finish him off,
with your light
with your holiest light!
O, Sir you will come in the morning's light
I no longer can see your holy light, your power.

Here in the *Talocan*
here in the house of darkness
I beseech you   this child   his spirit.
Here I offer you such prayers
here I let you have all my strength, my soul.
Where is this one?
Where is our child being kept?
Would you give him to me O, Sir?
O, Sir I beg of you.
Perhaps he has fallen,
perhaps he is standing.
Where do I search?
Where is he being kept?
Where is he?
Has he been taken from where he lowered his voice?
Has he been taken from where he prayed to you?
I ask nothing for myself.
Here I live well, a good life,
here I am sustained
here I am happy
I am satisfied with my life.
With such prayers I beseech you
I ask with such love
you sustain us, you give us life
I beseech you.
O, help me Sir!
They should be sent everywhere
they should search for him

they should find him
they should bring him to us.
Bring him to us!
Now I beseech you.
Give him to me!

All the Archangels will come
to save me with the morning's light,
save me with your light
take me in the morrow!
O, that I should see your light
They are holding him.
They are keeping him.
Let him be brought forth
let him be freed
let him come to you
let him be brought forth to you.
Our savior Jesus Christ grant this.
Saint Michael Archangel grant this.
Saint John Offshoot of God
Saint John of the Light
Saint John Morning star
Joseph, Mary, Trinity
Sir John Emanuel Anthony Marquis
Sir John Emanuel Martin Ocelo
Sir Manuel Antonio Francisco Hernandez
Sir Martín Antonio Francisco Abad
Saint James Cavalier
Miraculous General of Light
take me with the morning's light!
Let me see your holy light.

Thank you
many thanks
I thank you all, Sirs.
With all of my force
I say it.

Thank you our Savior.

Thank you lord of earth.

The prayers, such as in the above passage, constitute a template against which activities in the underworld are compared with those of the real world. They also provide a template for comparing the known world to the fundamental philosophical concepts essential within Nahua culture.

Taloc is the earth. He/she is the embodiment of *talocan*. He/she is the mother and father of humankind, which both sustains life and consumes it. The concept is fundamentally dualistic, yet in prayer this dualism is not a dichotomy but a fusion of the seemingly dichotomous elements. Just as the individual's life on the earth depends upon the beneficence of the sky and the earth, the most holy light, and the house of darkness that places the individual as the mediator of this supernatural dichotomy, the dualistic relationship must be resolved constantly in order to maintain and reproduce everyday life.

The relationships that humankind must maintain with the supernatural, as shown in prayers, is dualistic, beseeching, playing off, and threatening the supernaturals of both worlds. In this sense, life on the earth is a constant dialectic that is resolved each day. *Taloc* and *talocan* may sustain life on the earth, but it is humankind that maintains, with prayers and offerings, life of the earth.

This is a reciprocal relationship like most others maintained by villagers in everyday life. This is one of the fundamental types of relationship that is maintained by villagers in social, religious, and economic contexts, and without it, the networks of obligation in everyday life would cease to function. By maintaining his relationships to the world of the ancestors and traditions, man also provides a template for the relationships in the social world that sustain the interactions of everyday life. *Talocan* sustains and consumes humankind.

These prayers illustrate a characteristic leap of faith from the concepts, symbols, metaphors, and relationships to the world of everyday life. They constitute a template for the natural and social environment against which the activities of the known world of everyday life are compared. They are also the template against which direct personal experience of the unconscious and unknown world of the ancestors is compared in dreams.

The metalanguage of dreams manifested in the curer's dreamtales is a fusion of knowledge and practice that in a meaningful way seeks to interpret the actions of everyday life. This cultural reality is constantly being interpreted and reinterpreted in practical everyday life. There are so many interpretations, yet, as Todorov (1982b: 170) asks, "What position must one occupy in order to be capable of describing all interpretive strategies?" For people today in the Sierra de Puebla, life is interpreted as a fundamental balance between earth and sky, light and dark, known and unknown, natural and social environments, change and tradition. Life on the earth remains today a balancing act between the sustaining and consuming nature of *talocan,* the most holy earth.

The metalanguage of dreams that curers use to explain their experiences in the underworld of their ancestors is an attempt to make sense of the unconscious using these principles. When a curer recounts his or her dreams for a client, it is done in a way that brings to bear the knowledge and geography of the underworld fused with traditional philosophical concepts. The form, geography, and structure of the underworld and its inhabitants learned by practitioners is in a very real sense a map of the traditions of the ancestors.

CHAPTER FOUR

LIFE IN THE HOLY EARTH

*The Aztec Underworld in the Natural World
of the Sierra de Puebla, a Geography*

THE GEOGRAPHY OF THE UNDERWORLD is the practitioner's most important body of knowledge in dealing with clients. The process of learning the geography grounds the initiate in the fundamental principles and natural philosophy of the traditions of the ancestors. It provides him or her with the tools necessary to explain the traditions of the ancestors and the holy earth, *talocan*.

This is a unique system, though there are probably many similar systems in Mesoamerica. It is a coherent articulation of fundamental concepts, meanings, and metaphors (Knab 1984) characteristic of Mesoamerica as a cohesive cultural area. It is also an extension of the natural world into the realm of the supernatural: the interpretation of the unknown and unknowable from the known world.

In diagnostic dreams, native practitioners search out the cause of a client's problems in the underworld of the ancestors. The dreamtales are a metalanguage that allows practitioners to develop a dialogue with clients and their families that may have a multiplicity of meanings. A short and simple synopsis of a dream text will illustrate this concept:

First I found myself on a path in the hills, and I followed it. I followed it to a stream that entered into a cave. Inside the cave I could not cross the stream but on the other side there was a cornfield with tender ears of corn. I was hungry but couldn't cross the river. I put some large stepping stones into the river, but it carried them off. I still could not cross, so I decided to jump, and I leapt a huge distance. When I arrived at the other side I found that the ears of corn were dry, so I went to a well and brought them water. They revived and I ate them.

There were six possible interpretations of even this short dream that were all discussed by the curer, the client, and his family. The client's father believed that the new corn was clearly a trick by the *amotocnihuan* to lure more souls into the underworld. The client's aunt believed the dream meant that the curer would eventually find the client's soul because the corn came back to life and was edible. The third interpretation, by the client, was that the curer should not have crossed the stream because the corn was a trick. He also believed that his soul could not have been lost there because he was not foolish enough to try to cross such a stream. Other family members had their own interpretations of the dream, and after long discussion, this particular dream was determined to be inconclusive. The curer returned a few days later with another dream. Each dream is an exploration of the vague geography of the underworld, *talocan*, as much as it is an exploration of the problems of everyday life.

THE UNDERWORLD: ALTERNATE GEOGRAPHY

Talocan shares with our world on the surface of the earth such basic geographic characteristics as mountains, rivers, lakes, waterfalls, towns, and villages. There are cities such as Paris and Mexico City in the underworld. There is a great sea in the east and mountains in the west of *talocan*. At the center of the realm of darkness, there is even *talocan melauh,* a town too similar to San Martín for coincidence.

Although the geographical features of the underworld may parallel those of the surface of the earth, *talocan* is different. It is part of the world of dreams. It is the unknowable world of tradition that is visited almost daily. *Talocan* is a world of darkness. There are no real plants in *talocan*, for example. They need light, *nexti.* Yet, *talocan* provides the life-giving moisture and the spark of life that seeds require to sprout. It is the source of all that grows on the surface of the earth. It is the Most Holy Earth.

Things in *talocan* are obscure in many ways. *Talocan* is well known by native practitioners, yet unknown. For example, although it is said that there are no plants in the underworld, Doña Rubia and Don Inocente agree that there is a great tree in the center of the underworld, the *talcuauhuit* or *xochicuauhuit,* which supports the surface of the earth. The tree is fashioned of earth, rather than wood, and what look like leaves are the roots of plants we see on the surface of the earth. The branches are limestone formations that jut from the soil.[1]

According to Inocente, there are four other trees located at the four sides of the underworld that serve to support the four sides of the earth. Although Rubia and Inocente differ on this matter, they see no conflict in their interpretations or perceptions of the underworld, for it is a world of obscurity and darkness where many things may remain unseen in dreams. Contradictory views can be quite common, yet they cause the practitioners little problem, for in the realm of darkness many things may be obscured.

The geography of the underworld is a geography of the unknown, yet it is not idiosyncratic or arbitrary. The geography of *talocan* is a conceptual geography of great consistency.

The underworld, *talocan,* is not necessarily a world of perpetual night, but rather dusk or perpetual dense fogs such as those that envelop the village of San Martín much of the year. This foggy, obscure nature of *talocan* is extremely important. It permits native practitioners to recount their dreamtime travels from place to place in this world of darkness without ever fixing the spatial relationships among sites visited in the underworld. There are, thus, a huge number of geographical features of indeterminate location in the underworld. In fact, every place outside of the center of *talocan* and within the four sides that define the edges of the underworld[2] is of indeterminate location.

For the people of San Martín, as for the people of most small villages who rarely venture far from their homes, the town or village is a well-defined center. When moving out from the center, observable features are defined in relation to the center while those that are unobserved yet known are relegated to conceptual space and indefinite location (Gossen 1974: 16). Conceptual geography in this sense is based on belief, or confidence, in a particular natural philosophy. Even our own knowledge of the world around us is based for the most part on our confidence in our own system of natural philosophy.

Given the vague undefined nature of the underworld, the metalanguage of dreams becomes a vehicle for expressing, speculating, and interpreting the nature of the world around us. None of the native practitioners can in fact specify if traveling from one place to another in the underworld requires passing through a series of fixed places with consistent spatial relationships. In the obscure, foggy underworld, such matters are of little import.

It is often said that:

In *talocan* there is no holy light.
In *talocan* there is not the light of day.
In *talocan* there is not the glory of the sun.
In *talocan* things are not CLEEEARLY seen.
In *talocan* things are neither here nor there,
neither the near nor the neigh is clearly seen.

As a place of darkness or shadows, *talocan* is not a region easily remembered, and special training or assistance is required of dreamers to recall the events occurring in the underworld. Curers must struggle to wrest their recollections from the obscurity of dreams, the shadows of *talocan*. The training of a native practitioner in dreams consists essentially of recounting and interpreting dreams until the events wrested from the obscurity of the unconscious can be described in terms of the places and events possible in the underworld, i.e., until the metalanguage of dreams is learned and the initiate learns to tell a dreamtale. Learning the metalanguage is a metaphoric struggle, just as the process of curing a client is a metaphoric struggle with the supernaturals of the underworld to restore the client's soul to the harmonious balance necessary for life on earth. It is only with great difficulty and training that practitioners can bring forth their knowledge of the underworld.

In prayers the lords of the underworld are often cajoled into parting with their council in this way:

O, Lord *Taloc*!
O, Lady *Taloc*!
Recount to me these things!
Grant to me your knowing words!

O, that I may take them with me,
that I may bear them on my shoulders
with great labor and much difficulty
to this poor one, your child.
O, I beseech you this,
I ask you with such great love and affection
with so many prayers!
Give this to me!
Now, you must give it to me!

The obscure nature of *talocan* presents another problem in interpretation of the underworld, in that there may be multiple interpretations of
the same phenomena that are equally correct, coherent, and acceptable.
This can cause considerable difficulty in explanation or exposition for a
non-Nahua audience, yet for native practitioners multiple interpretations
are highly valued. For example, features of indeterminate location are
often described in ways that will make them appear layerings, different
levels of the underworld, as follows:

I entered through the third[3] great cave mouth at the second great
river and searched the path along the river full of brambles and
thorns until I came to the second great highway. It was a *camino
real,* royal highway, that I followed to the second small hill. There,
were there those others, the *talocanca.* I went to the third great
river. I searched the path along the river full of brambles and thorns
until I came to the third great highway. It too was a royal highway
and I followed it to the third small hill. There were *talocanca* there
just as before. I went to the fifth great river, the same as the others,
all together, the various places. I searched the path along the river
full of thorns and brambles until I came to the fifth great highway,
a royal highway. At the fifth small hill I heard it. I heard the name
of Fulano[4]. It was them. It was the *talocanca* who called him. I hid
on the third small hill to see them. They searched the fifth small
hill. They called out to Fulano. They spoke of Fulano. Then the rat
screamed. The third small hill rat who lived there saw me. And they
came, those others came, those who are not our brothers came after
me. Those *talocanca* came. And I went, I split, I vamoosed out of
there, through the gateway into the light.

Both practitioners described the events in this dream as going deeper and further into the underworld, and one explicitly stated that these places were one on top of one another. This appears at least to imply the existence of different levels within the underworld, yet neither of the practitioners liked the notion of levels when I presented it to them. Doña Rubia said that there could be levels like I had described to her, but it was always too foggy in *talocan,* when she was there, to see the levels. The underworld is not conceived of as a plane with features scattered over it nor as a series of planes, but rather as a center with four sides defining a world with vast indeterminate regions.

Though spatial relationships and levels may be implied among features and separate regions may appear distinguishable, all but the defining features are shrouded in the mists of obscurity in the underworld. Dreams relocate and rearrange the indeterminate geographic features of the underworld, and each dream is a new search for meaning in the darkness of *talocan.* The only places of fixed definite location in the underworld are those that define the geography of *talocan*: the axis and four sides. The initiate must discover in his or her dreams all of these places before actually being considered a curer.

THE AXIS WITH FOUR SIDES[5]

In *talocan* there are essentially five regions with fixed spatial relationships. These five locations define not only *talocan* but the conceptual universe: the sky, the underworld, and the earth upon which life exists. These five places form the limits of both the known world and the worlds that are unknowable. They are viewed as a flower and referred to as the *talocan xochit, flor de talocan,* or underworld flower (see Figure 4). Though these places may not often be mentioned in the metalanguage of dreams, they are key points that must be understood fully. They are the essential boundaries of the universe that native practitioners must learn in order to orient themselves in their dreamtime journeys to the realm of the unknown. Before a native practitioner can develop concepts about the underworld, it is essential that the limits of that world be known. These are the key points that define the social, conceptual, and symbolic worlds.

The fundamental importance of these definite locations is that they fix the most important point in the conceptual universe, the center, *talocan melauh,* 'the true *talocan.*' This is where the lords of the underworld are

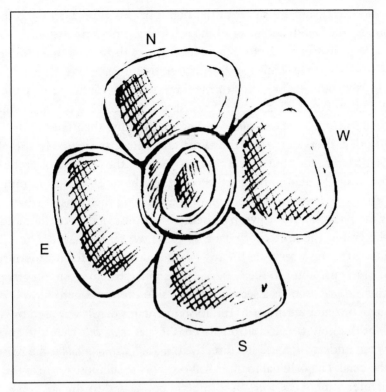

Figure 4. The talocan *flower: a mapping of the underworld.*

to be found. This is the most potent symbolic point in the underworld. Not unexpectedly, the central axis of the underworld reflects the central axis of people's everyday lives, the village of San Martín, in its structure and form. It is a mapping of the supernatural from the natural world.

The four sides of the underworld are perhaps better considered as domains of all things associated with each particular side of *talocan*. The inhabitants of these domains define the relationships that exist between earth and sky, as well as earth and underworld. The four sides define the edges of the conceptual universe where earth, *talticpac,* sky, *ilhuicac,* and underworld, *talocan,* meet.

The east and the west are the exit and entryway, respectively, for the sun as it passes from underworld to sky on its constant journey from night to day. In the south is the source of heat, which is also identified with the zenith or hottest part of the day, and the north, the source of chilling winds and death, is the place identified with midpoint of night, the coldest and most dangerous part of the night. In this sense, north and south represent the zenith and nadir of the celestial journey, and the north–south plane appears twisted at the axis, rotated ninety degrees, representing heat and cold as well as zenith and nadir (see figure 2).

In the south is the point of maximum heat or light, *nexti,* which is often glossed as 'holy grace' in Spanish when referring to light's super-natural role in the heavens, *ilhuicac.* The south is thus the position for deal-ing with matters of the sky, the saints, and Christian deities. In the plaza of San Martín, the church, the primary focus of the public cult of the sky and saints, is located in the southern section, the point of maximum light or 'grace.' In the northern section of the plaza are the ruins of what once was the *presidencia,* or town hall, before the construction of the building at the end of the nineteenth century that now serves that function. The building that now serves as the town hall is also within the northern por-tion of the plaza just to the west of the original structure. An integral part of the old *presidencia* is a section on one side that appears to have been a *temascal* or Aztec steam bath. Tradition maintains that it was used by offi-cials at the new year. Tradition also has it that *temascals* were the entries into the underworld and led directly to *mictalli* or *miquitalan,* the regions of the dead. The original town hall also served as jailhouse for many years, and, interestingly, the *temescal* is directly connected to the jail cell.[6]

To the east of the plaza stretches the coastal plain, which on a clear day blends in the distance with the blue–green waters of the Gulf of Mex-ico. In the west, the village is ringed by mountains, each taller than the next, up to the Mexican central highlands. The plaza of San Martín is in this sense a microcosm of the world as a whole as well as a model for the makeup of *talocan.* The natural world, viewed from the center of San Martín, is the model to which the sky and underworld are compared. It embodies the natural phenomena and events that together form the basis for the natural philosophy that relates humankind to the natural world in Mesoamerica (see Figure 5, p. 115) and has done so for centuries.[7]

In the process of training native curers, it is essential that the novice know the four sides of the underworld. Immediately after the initiation, when the novice has spent an entire night praying at the mouth of a cave to the lords of the underworld, making offerings and sacrifices, the real process of training begins. The initiate must begin to recount all of his or her dreams. The dreams are analyzed and discussed with a seasoned practitioner, who interprets and reinterprets their multiple shades of meaning and the subtleties of the soul's dreamtime journeys in the underworld.

In the first few dreams, the initiate learns to direct his *itonal,* that aspect of the soul that travels through dream time. There are several factors that direct the soul in dream time. The first is autosuggestion and perhaps a desire to please the practitioner. The second is the growing body of knowledge of the underworld gained from long sessions of analysis with a trained practitioner. There are also techniques of sympathetic magic and specific offerings that may be used to direct the soul. Should all else fail, pilgrimages and long vigils in caves, near streams and pools, or on mountaintops are used to direct the soul.

The form and structure of the underworld is passed to the initiate in a helter-skelter way that at first makes little sense. As this process continues, the initiate begins to synthesize, to make sense out of a growing knowledge of the underworld. This is done on the basis of commonsense knowledge of everyday life in the natural and social environment. Basic assumptions, metaphors, and meanings begin to shape the initiate's knowledge of the underworld and the proper interpretation of dreams.

As the initiate's knowledge of the underworld grows and the ability to interpret and direct dreams becomes more acute, the practitioner explains the necessity of finding the four sides of the underworld and seeking out allies, additional animal alter egos, in the underworld. If the initiate's dreams do not lead to the four sides of the underworld in a reasonable time, various rituals are prescribed that are different for men and women. The rituals depend on the particular initiate and assist in the process of discovering the edges of the conceptual universe. The novice must find the four sides of the underworld before searching out its center.

According to both practitioners, it is impossible to find the 'true *talocan,'* talocan melauh, the center of the underworld, before knowing the four sides of the underworld. Should the initiate find the center of the underworld before knowing the four sides, he or she probably would not recognize it, and the lords of the underworld would likely keep the initiate's *itonal* in the underworld, causing sickness and possibly death.

Without a knowledge of the four sides of the underworld for orientation the soul can become easily lost in dreams. The four sides are the four major passages from the underworld to the world of humankind, and, although there are many other techniques of passage and points of passage in the underworld, these four points act as emergency exits in fixed positions.

In the initial dreams during training, the novice must seek out an entry to the underworld. This may be a cave, it may be behind the altar or behind the church of San Martín, it may be in a well or alongside a stream. It is both a real place in the waking world and a place that the initiate has dreamt. The initiate is encouraged to leave offerings at dusk and dawn at these entryways to *talocan*. A knowledgeable practitioner may have dozens of entryways to the underworld where offerings are left before beginning to cure a client.

The entry to the underworld is of primary symbolic importance in analysis of dreams. It determines the tone of the dream. Entering the underworld in the water or with the winds is far more auspicious than climbing or crawling into *talocan*. Being shown an entry by one of the supernaturals of the underworld is considered especially auspicious. Although any soul can travel to the underworld in dreams, it is only the trained practitioner who can direct his or her *itonal* through specific entries and exits. In some instances, a curer may be chased from the underworld by a witch or one of the residents of the underworld, or may even be banished from the underworld by one of its lords. In such cases, the practitioner must flee from one of the four sides of the underworld.

It is not necessary for the initiate to find the four sides of the underworld in any specific order, but all four must be located before entry into the center of *talocan*. Once initiated, a novice must take special care to leave proper offerings at each of the entries that is found in training. This can become an arduous task, and an expensive one, if too many entries are found. Conceptually, however, these points are far less important than the four sides of *talocan*.

FOUR REGIONS OF DARKNESS

The North: Cold Winds and Death

In the North of *talocan* are the places called *mictan*, *miquitalli*, or *miquitallan*, the place of the dead, the cemetery, and *ehecatan* or *ehecatallan*, the place of the winds or world of winds. Opinions concerning this side of the underworld are highly divergent, and in some cases even contradictory. The two practitioners with whom I studied not only described this side of the underworld differently, but had very different opinions as to the malevolence or danger associated with the places found here.

According to one of the practitioners, the cave of the winds is the gateway to *miquitalli*. According to the other, the cemetery is the only possible entryway to the land of the dead, and the cave of the winds is simply the source of all winds. It has little or no relation to the land of the dead. They are simply two parallel places in the northern reaches of the underworld. The two practitioners appear to agree that the north is a region of intense cold and profound darkness. It is the source of the winds that bring death along with them into the world of the living.

Given the geographic location of San Martín in the northern reaches of the Sierra de Puebla, it is a logical conclusion that the north would be the source of cold and death. In the cold season from November to March, the chilling northern winds (called *nortes* in Spanish) can bring snow and ice to the region, wreaking great damage on crops and bringing sickness and death. Intense periods of cold can be devastating for people subsisting on a meager diet and accustomed to a semitropical climate.

The dominant supernaturals in this realm are the *ehecatagat,* the lord of the winds, and the *miquitagat,* the lord of death. They are the ones who care for souls for the first year after death. Both of the lords live in great caves. One of the practitioners maintains that they live in the same cave with two parts, while the other believes that there are two caves, one on top of the other, and that death lives in the lowest realm. The dead enter the underworld from the cemetery, where the lord death and his minions keep their souls. The role of the lord of the winds is to seek out more souls on the surface of the earth with which to populate the regions of the dead.

The underworld, *talocan,* is both the provider of life on the surface of the earth and its ultimate consumer. A common way in which people express their attitude toward this aspect of the Most Holy Earth is this:

We eat of the earth,
and then the earth eats us.

From the cave of the winds in the northern reaches of *talocan* issue the *mal aires* or evil winds, the feared *ahmo cualli ehecat,* the *sombra de muerte* or shadow of death, *miquicihual* and the *miquiehecat,* the *nortes,* 'the winds of death.' All these things are sent forth on the surface of the earth by the lords of these northern reaches of the underworld to seek out the souls of the living and bring them into the world of the dead. These lords of the north must continually repopulate their domain with the souls of the living. Thus they are responsible for much of the sickness, suffering, and death on the surface of the earth.

Once the dead are buried, they begin to take on the appearance of the lord death, who is nothing but bone. One of the curers is of the opinion that lord death eats the flesh from the dead when they are buried and feeds the flesh that is left to the minions of the north who have a particular craving for human flesh. Should the supernaturals of the north escape the underworld they would become cannibals on the surface of the earth. Though they may look like other people, they have a passion for human flesh. In one dream account, a practitioner whose *inahual,* a coatimundi, is being pursued by the minions of the north, shouts at them:

> Jaguars! People eaters! Eaters of the dead!
> Leave me! I run from you!
> Vultures! Strippers and cutters of flesh!
> I live! I run!
> Chichimecs[8]! Cannibals! Butchers!
> Leave me! I live!
> Go eat the dead!
>
> And then,
> then I slipped through a small hole,
> I went inside (the tree where he had been running)
> into the sun
> on   the earth
> in the holy light.
> I got out of there, I escaped.
> Whhheᵉᵉeₑₑw! They left me!

The cave of the winds is where the storms that ravage the land take shape. It is a place of smoke and mist, winds and tempests. It is where the lord of the winds resides with his various assistants who guard the cooking pots where the ingredients for storms are kept, the winds, mists, rains, thunder, and lightning.[9] Other assistants of the lord of the winds are the *quauhtiomeh* or lightning bolts, the thunderclaps or *popocameh,* and the smoke ones, who make the *miquipopoca* or smoke of death that issues forth onto the surface of the earth, *in talticpac,* along with the winds of death. Normally the *popocameh* are found in the south of the underworld, but some assist the lord of the winds and lord death in the north as they seek new souls to populate the regions of darkness.

The cave of the winds is reputed to be one of the most difficult places in the underworld to enter due to the constant, strong, and dangerous winds it emits. There are constant cold winds that come from the limestone caves around San Martín, even in the warmest weather. These winds are considered to be extremely dangerous. One always smokes tobacco when passing near the caves to ward off the supernaturals of the underworld (Knab 1978). The winds of the cave carry with them the danger of death.

Despite the fact that native practitioners do not agree on the exact location of the land of the dead and the cave of the winds, the logical association of wind and death in the north makes them seem to be two parallel and complementary worlds. Beliefs concerning the cave of the winds are also intimately associated with witchcraft, and it is said that the most effective witches in the twenties and thirties in the War of the Witches went there to do their evil deeds.

The South: The Infernal Fires

The south is a place of heat often referred to in Nahuat as *atotonican* and in Spanish as *infierno,* the inferno. There are some in San Martín who would associate the south of the underworld with the fires of hell in the land of the dead. This is probably an extension of the Spanish gloss of this region that confuses Western and traditional concepts. Native practitioners are quite clear that this is not a place of torment for lost souls. It is not the Christian hell or even a syncretic analog of it. Descriptions of the southern reaches of the underworld make it quite clear that the realm is part of a fundamentally Mesoamerican cosmovision that is based on a natural philosophy integrating the natural world with the supernatural.

The south is also a region of darkness in the underworld, but it is more like a land of perpetual dusk illuminated by the eternal fires that heat the region and obscured by their smoke. The central feature of the region is a spring of boiling water shrouded in steam and clouds. This spring is found in the depths of a cave illuminated by the fires of the *popocameh.*

In the depths of this boiling spring, according to one of the practitioners, lives a fantastic monster, said to be like a giant worm, the *cuiluhuexi.*

The *cuiluhuexi* eats the earth and fashions the caverns that permeate its surface. Its fiery breath and boiling saliva eat away the earth as it crawls beneath the surface. The other practitioner sees the spring itself as the mouth of the *cuiluhuexi* or *huey ocuillin* and the boiling waters as its saliva.

The lord or master of this region of *talocan* is the *cuiluhuexi,* which appears to be a fearsome earth monster forever hollowing out caves and grottos beneath the surface of the earth. All the fires and heat that bubble forth on the surface of the earth come from its depths. All heat that springs forth from the earth "without light of day or grace of sun" has as its origin *talocan* and is a danger for mankind.

In the following prayer, a practitioner sends an ally to search for a lost soul in the south of the underworld:

> Go! To the source of fires, the unholy fires,
> the heat that has not seen face of day
> heat without holy light
> the fires of the evil ones.
> And *search* there among the fires for THOSE
> those who are not our brothers
> those without the holy light, without face of day
> those who guard the FIRES
> those who eat the earth, who heat the earth.

When seeking the cause of an illness associated with heat, a practitioner will often first search the realms of the south. Any illness that produces heat in the body, even ones that are clearly classified as organic, may be the result of some offense or some form of witchcraft directed from the southern reaches of the underworld.

For practitioners, the south is not a place of the dead, yet it is a place of mortal danger for the soul. A wide range of illnesses are attributed to the *popocameh,* and when making offerings at the cave, *aguardiente* and red flowers are always included for the supernaturals of this part of the underworld.

The East: The Great Seas of the Underworld

In the east is the place known as *apan,* the waters, and it is from there that the sun leaves the underworld to begin its daytime journey over the surface of the earth bringing mankind its holy light. *Apan* is a great lake or sea in the underworld that is united in its depths with all the waters of the surface of the world. In its depths live the *atagat* and the *acihuat,* the lord and lady of the waters. The *acihuat* is often identified with the *llorona* or weeping woman of folklore, who, in the Sierras at least, is always found near sources of water weeping for her lost children.

Beneath the surface of the underworld waters live not only the lord and lady of the waters, but all of the supernaturals associated with the waters (Knab 1978). In the depths of *apan* are cities, fields, villages, and gardens of great abundance. The fields and gardens of this region require no labor; they simply continue to produce all the fruits, grains, and vegetables that could be desired. For this reason, souls—once they have passed out of the north at the end of the first year of death—seek out the abundance of this region.

All the waters of the earth eventually become a part of this region, and the masters of the waters control not only all of the waters of the underworld but also those of the surface. The 'water man' and 'water woman,' who rule this realm, can be both benevolent and terrifying at the same time. The waters of the underworld are heavily populated with the souls of the dead as well as other supernaturals, many of whom actively seek more souls on the surface of the earth, causing disease and death. A practitioner searching for a lost soul must, however, seek it out beneath the waters of the underworld as a last resort. The lord and lady of this region will take the curer's soul if the effort has not already been made to find the soul in all other parts of the underworld.

Apan is considered the most difficult place in the underworld to recapture a lost soul. It is a place of plenty, a place of abundance, and few souls after they have seen its bounty wish to return to the waking world of suffering and deprivation. The practitioner must convince and cajole souls lost in the waters to return, or must with offerings and prayers beseech the masters of this realm to return lost souls. Often a practitioner must enlist allies in the underworld to assist in the recapture of a soul from this region, beseeching them with offerings for their aid and paying them regularly afterwards with offerings or by indenturing the client to them.

Apan is the source of all maladies associated with the water, whether they be organic in nature or maladies of the spirit. Should an individual have an *inagual,* or animal alter ego, associated with the water—a fish, frog, turtle, salamander, etc.—then it is to *apan* that the curer must journey to see that the *inagual* is well and has not been captured by some witch.

The West: Mountains of the Sun

In the west is the place referred to as *tonallan*. This is where the mountain is found that the sun stops at on its daily journey before descending into the underworld. This mountain, the *talocan tepet,* reaches from the depths of the underworld to the sky. Like the great sea in the east, which is united with all the waters of the world, this mountain is part of the endless chain of western mountains. It is on this mountain that the *cihuauhchan,* or house of women, is found. One of the practitioners, Inocente, maintained that this is actually a cave inhabited only by truly dangerous women such as the *miquicihuauh,* 'death woman,' and the *ehecacihuauh,* 'wind woman.' The *acihuauh,* or 'water woman,' often identified in Spanish as the *llorona,* also inhabits the *cihuauhchan.*

The *miquicihuauh* is charged with the care of the souls of women in the *cihuauhchan.* The souls of women who have died search throughout the underworld for the *cihuauhchan,* for this is a house where they have no work. There is no cleaning, cooking, weaving, or washing to do in the *cihuauhchan.* This is a woman's paradise.

The wind woman, *ehecacihuauh,* unlike her counterpart in the north, the *ehecatagat,* who looses the fearsome winds and storms that bring death in their wake, is charged with the sweet moist winds that bring rain for the crops, the gentle mists and soft breezes. These winds may also take souls as they pass gently over the Sierras. Souls, especially those of women, are seduced by the soft and gentle winds into abandoning a life of toil and uncertainty on the surface of the earth. These souls are among the most difficult to recover from the underworld, for they willingly leave life on the surface of the earth. Both practitioner and client must bargain for the return of these reluctant souls.

Inocente always maintained that the women from this side of the underworld were extremely dangerous. Should one come upon them at night, along a path or near a well, pool, or stream, it would be certain death. These women would not return the souls of men. At night, they went in search of the souls of men, especially lascivious men who couple with various women. They would also take the souls of women waiting on the paths, in the gardens, or in the fields for their illicit lovers. There was no hope for those who encountered these women. Their entire soul, all three aspects, was taken directly into the underworld never again to see the light of day.

The western entry to the underworld is where the sun is captured each day to begin its passage through *talocan*. This gateway is unlike the entry of the east through the waters, which may be used at any time for a practitioner's dreamtime escape from or passage to *talocan*. This gateway may only be used after midnight, for otherwise it would be too hot due to the passage of the sun. The women of the west seek the sun and at the same time are constantly watching for any soul passing through their domain. This makes passage through the western portals of the underworld at all times extremely dangerous for dreamers. Both practitioners recounted great battles to escape *talocan* from this side.

On all four sides, the sky, the underworld, and the surface of the earth are united. Thus, these are the limits of the cosmos. These limits correspond in a real way to the natural limits, seen from the Sierras, of the known world. To the east and west, the perceived world is limited by the sea and the mountains, respectively. To the north and south, the limits are more conceptual, heat and cold, which are yet reflections of the natural environment.

The conceptual center of San Martín, its plaza, and the conceptual center of *talocan,* the true heart of the underworld, *talocan melauh,* share many of the same characteristics. The conceptual center of the Aztec Empire, the Templo Mayor, likewise demonstrated a coherent Mesoamerican cosmovision (Carrasco 1990: 51) shared by many other sites. Many of the same fundamental features of Mesoamerican cosmovision based on a coherent natural philosophy (Broda 1987: 126; 1991: 111) can be shown for modern manifestations of the sacred center of the Most Holy Earth, *talocan,* in the Sierra de Puebla today.

TALOCAN MELAUH: THE TRUE HEART OF DARKNESS

Talocan melauh, the true center of the world of darkness, the hub of the four sides of the earth, the pivot of the underworld, is the central axis of existence both in the earth and on the earth. It is not only the geographical center of the underworld but the social, political, and symbolic center as well. The center of the underworld is where all of the lords and officials of the underworld reside and where most of the supernaturals who populate the underworld come for their existence. It is where blood and water are the same.

In the very center of the underworld there is a plaza with a 'church' for the denizens of darkness on the southern end and the municipal palace in the north, the same arrangement as in the village of San Martín Zinacapan. The center of *talocan* is the center of both civil and religious, public and private life in the underworld. It is the center of both power and authority. In this sense, the events in the center of the underworld control the very existence of life on the surface of the earth (see figure 5).

The *presidencia,* the town hall and capital of *talocan,* is a building with three doors and three rooms. The center room is for the lords of the underworld. The room on the west side of the building is for the civil officials of the underworld: the president, mayor, treasurer, judges, executioners and their assistants. The eastern room is for the religious officials of the underworld who care for and cater to the true *taloc,* arranging his festivals, bearing her offerings, and caring for the source of all life in the earth. Unlike the old *presidencia* in the plaza of San Martín, the doors of this building do not open onto the central plaza but rather away from it.

Opposite the municipal palace of the underworld is the 'church' of *talocan.* As one of the practitioners explained, "This is not a church like all others with a cross and a bell tower; it is a cave that leads deep down below the center of the plaza. It is there that 'those others,' those of *talocan* go to pray." This cave is where the true *taloc, taloc melauh,* the animate embodiment of all the underworld, the lord of this realm of darkness[10] resides. The true *taloc* is the same as the lords of the underworld who reside in the palace. The true *taloc* is the *taloc totatzin,* and the *taloc tonantzin, taloc* the great father, and *taloc* the great mother. The true *taloc* is also the *Señor taloc* and the *Señora taloc,* the lord and lady *taloc.* The true *taloc* is in fact, in a sense, the embodiment of all the lords of the underworld.

Although the mother/father, lord/lady *taloc* appear distinct from the 'true *taloc,*' they are in the words of the practitioners "the same thing." The 'true *taloc,*' who lives in the depths of the cave under the central plaza of the underworld, is in fact never seen, for within this cave the darkness is total.

The appearance of the 'true *taloc*' is pure speculation, but one of the practitioners conjectured that its eyes must be immense like those of other denizens of the darkness. Perhaps the great, round eyes seen throughout Teotihuácan (the largest city in Mesoamerica in the Classic period 200–600 A.D., whose ruins lie just outside Mexico City) also come from the inhabitants of the nocturnal world. Another of the prac-

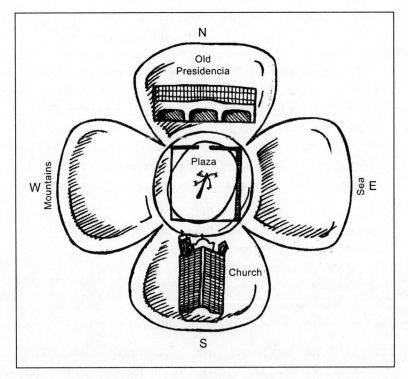

Figure 5. The center of San Martín and the heart of the underworld: natural and supernatural geography.

titioners speculated that "perhaps *taloc* would have teeth like a toad[11], since those are the things that live there (in the cave)." Someone else commented that the lords of the underworld look like ordinary people only a bit larger.

In the center of the plaza of *talocan* there is a well, much like the one behind the plaza that all the women of San Martín used for water before the present-day system of piping was installed. From this pool spring forth all the waters of the world, and it is there that the *atagat* and *acihuat* live when they are in the center of the underworld. From this well there is a small current that seeps back into the cave where the *taloc melauh* resides. One of the curers maintains that the well is filled with blood and that it is a river of blood that flows out of the well and into the mouth of the waiting *taloc melauh,* whom they identify as a vampire-like toad. (All cave toads are considered vampires because they are generally blamed for the nasty insect bites one suffers around the ankles when one enters a cave.)

Also in the center of the underworld is the great tree that supports the surface of the earth. Despite the fact that opinions concerning the tree are quite diffuse and confusing (and neither of the practitioners with whom I trained remember having seen it in their dreamtime travels in the underworld), both practitioners insist that it is located in the center of the underworld. Rubia insisted that it grew from the center of the plaza in *talocan,* whereas Inocente insisted that it grew to one side of the palace. He also insisted that there were four other trees, one at each of the four sides of the underworld, which grew from the earth to the sky.

In his prayers, he mentioned the tree incessantly, often in this way:

Take me there to your tree of the death
Take me there to your tree of the waters
Take me there to your fuming tree
Take me there to the Sun's tree
Take me there into your holy light
Take me there with all of your force
Take me with your most holy light, with your most holy force

Except for these two practitioners, I found no one in the area who knew anything about an underworld tree. In all of the stories and tales that I collected, there was nothing to speak of concerning this matter. Aramoni (1990: 176–95) does mention the tree and provides extensive documentation of its importance in Classic Aztec literature.

The 'true *talocan*' is the center of power in the underworld. From there, the officials of the underworld direct the activities of its inhabitants, religious officials organize festivities celebrating the lords of the underworld, and all the lords of the underworld exercise their sway not only over the underworld but also over the surface of the earth. It is the officials of *talocan* who command the minions of darkness and send them forth to search for souls of the living on the surface of the earth. It is also the officials of the underworld who hold the vigil that keeps captured souls in the underworld. The *aguaciles,* executioners, and *alcaldes,* jailers, as well as the guards and the armies of darkness seek to keep captured souls in the underworld. A practitioner must often do battle with these supernaturals in order to recover a lost soul.

All of the officials of the underworld are considered *taloques.* They inhabit all parts of the underworld and have power over other inhabitants of the underworld. They directly serve the lords of darkness as officials, assistants, and flunkies. If a practitioner must search out a lost soul, these same officials can be sought out in the center of the underworld and asked to assist in the search for a lost soul (provided the proper offerings are produced).

The officials of the underworld are its administrators. They determine, for example, the amount of water that is loosed on the surface of the earth. The lords of the underworld send their wishes via the *taloques* throughout the underworld. These officials also control the fertility of plants and the fecundity of animals. In this sense, the center of the underworld is the control center not only for the underworld but for the world of mankind as well.

THROUGH THE DARK MISTS: THE INDETERMINATE GEOGRAPHY OF *TALOCAN*

With the exception of the four sides and the center of the underworld, almost all of the rest of the features of *talocan* are of indeterminate location. They have no fixed spatial relationship to one another or to the fixed points of the underworld. The vast majority of the places found in dream-time journeys to the underworld are of indeterminate location. In general, these places reflect the geographical features of the known world, the surface of the earth inhabited by mankind. As in the waking world, there are rivers, streams, lakes, wells, and waterfalls; there are hills, mountains, forests, and cliffs; there are fields and plains, roads and highways, villages and cities. There are also a few features that do not appear on the surface of the earth. In Spanish, they are generally referred to as *encantos* or 'enchanted places.' In Nahuat these places are referred to specifically as the *tepeyolomeh*, 'hill hearts,' *atemeh*, 'water stones' or 'ice places,' and *ehecatzin*, wind places or 'windy ways.' The enchanted places are inhabited by animate beings of the same name and crop up in dreams only when especially important events take place or important places are visited.

One of the key points in the following dream searching for the lost soul of a twelve-year-old boy diagnosed with magical fright is the hill hearts. The practitioner entered the underworld through the mouth of a cave after a long journey through a dense forest. Once inside the cave, she could see nothing and stumbled constantly on the rough, rocky path. She found herself on a precipice with a waterfall, but it was still too dark to see anything.

There was the sound of the water and there were voices down below. I heard they were talking and I went down the steep path into the hill heart. They were talking and they did not see me at first. I said to them, I beseeched them for the soul of Juanito.

And then they said to me that it was not kept in any of the hill hearts of *talocan*. It was not in any of the great caves. It was not in any of the deep sink holes, and it was not being kept in any of the great mountains. They had not seen this soul but they would let me see with the eyes of a bird throughout *talocan* to search for the soul of Juanito.

At this point, the explanation of the dream told for the family of the client differed considerably from the version told to me. Rubia told me that she could "see with the dove" one of her animal alter egos, *inagual,* and that she then flew off throughout the underworld. For the client and his family, she did not identify the bird or mention that it was her *nonagual,* and she specifically stated that the *tepeyolomeh* made her into a bird.[12]

They would give me the wings of a bird to take me throughout *talocan*. They would let me fly to the four sides of the underworld. They would let me see everywhere in the world of darkness. They did this for me. They gave me this bird and it flew off to the forests. From the tops of the trees it could see nothing. It flew through the forests along the edges of the streams, everywhere on the great highways, everywhere on the small highways, on all the paths, on all the forest paths. It flew on wherever Juanito may walk in the darkness.

When Rubia finished explaining the dream, she and the client's family got into a long discussion of where the boy's soul could have been lost in the underworld, where he went on the surface of the earth, and where he would go in the underworld. She told the family to place flowers and water as offerings for the *tepeyolomeh*[13] on their household altar or near the cave. The next time she dreamed for the client, she found the boy's lost soul at the bottom of a deep ravine. She told the boy's father and his uncles that they should find a deep ravine and teach the boy to climb out of it so that his *itonal* could do the same in the underworld in dreamtime. The boy was cured.

Each type of feature found in the underworld exists in fourteen forms in fourteen places. For example, there are fourteen deep wells, fourteen waterfalls, fourteen lakes, fourteen dams, fourteen plains, fourteen corn, fields, fourteen highways, etc. These places are distributed throughout the underworld without any fixed relationship to one another. One can go from the first village to the sixth river to the fifth cornfield. In dreams, all places are accessible from all other places in the underworld. This is one of two essential qualities that makes the infinitely flexible meta-language of dreams such an important vehicle for curing. The other is the fact that the vague and obscure experiences of dreams can be described to the client in multiple ways, and it's up to the practitioner to choose the most meaningful way for each client.

The system of differentiating places of the same type, such as the first, second, and third rivers of the underworld, is rarely used by modern prac-titioners in explaining dreamtime experiences to clients. Both Rubia and Inocente insisted that I learn it, and both used it when discussing dreams with each other. I was never able to fully understand or appreciate the sys-tem, although Rubia especially tried to explain it to me and used it in almost every dream she told me, even in places and situations where it would not be necessary. Inocente did not emphasize the system as much, but he did insist that in the time of his parents and grandparents, every-one knew that places were luckier and more important depending on whether they were first, fourth, etc.

Today practitioners use the system when they pass through several places of the same type in a single dream, to differentiate one from another. For example, a practitioner may pass through the fifth river, then pass through another set of places, and return to the fifth river. Or he may pass through the fifth river, then pass through the third river, and then through the first river. The numeric classifiers simply help him distinguish different places of the same category. The other function of the numeric classifiers is to show the prominence or importance of a particular place in the underworld in a dreamtale. When the fifth river is the only place mentioned in a particular account, for example, it gives that feature increased prominence.

The meaning of the numeric classifiers is more than a bit problematic. Rubia always maintained that the number represented the distance from the center of the underworld. The higher the number, the closer to the center (and thus the more important).

All of the features of the underworld were said to exist in the center of the underworld, the 'true *talocan*.' There are thus thirteen of each type of feature located between the center and the edges of the underworld and one of each type of feature located in the center of the underworld.

Although it is possible that this system was at one time associated with the ritual divinatory calendar common throughout Mesoamerica, which features thirteen classes of twenty day names, the calendric system no longer exists in the Sierra de Puebla so this would only be a remote vestige of it. There is the possibility that the numeric system was just what it appears to be now, a way for specialists to clarify dreamtime accounts.

Given that the vast majority of the places visited in dreams are of indeterminate location, it is only natural that the way in which the experience and interpretation of dreams is structured is likewise vague and diffuse. The nebulous nature of dreamtime experience allows the curer, the client, and any others hearing the dream account to begin the process of interpretation in terms of their own experience. It allows them to project their own experience onto the dreamtale.

In this sense, the dream functions like a divinatory casting of lots, the *I Ching*, for example, or a Rorschach test encouraging all participants to project onto the dream their own emotions, fears, hopes, and feelings. Deep-seated emotions, motivations, and fears are often brought out in the discussion of dreams.

The stage for this social ritual is set when the practitioner begins to discuss a case with a client and the client's family. When the curer requests that specific ritual offerings be brought and begins to pray at the altar, he or she is setting the stage for recounting the dream. Then the practitioner begins to seek a dream. The prayers are the templates against which the dreamtime experience is measured, and the dreamtale becomes a projective mechanism.

Before beginning to dream for a client, a practitioner will pray. And though the prayer is only vaguely heard, it is a mysterious and wondrous thing for villagers who possess only a few notions of the supernatural world around them. The prayers empower the practitioners to search out in dreams the cure of a client's maladies.

Often the curer will seek out the aid of the inhabitants of the underworld in a prayer sending them forth to search out a client's lost soul.

Search for THIS, his lost soul!
If it is there among the fourteen deep green rivers,
    if it is there among the fourteen streams,

if it is there among the fourteen sandy streams,
if it is there among the fourteen huge hill hearts . . .
SEARCH IT OUT! If it should be in the fourteen deep holes,
in the fourteen deep canyons,
in the fourteen deep wells . . .
Perhaps it is there [in the underworld] that the vigil is kept [for
    this lost soul].
Perhaps it is there at one of the fourteen entryways to the
    underworld;
Perhaps it is there on one of the fourteen highways of the
    underworld . . .
WHERE does this lost soul rest?
WHERE is its vigil kept?

There are specific conventions as to the organization of the places in the underworld that are mentioned in prayers. For example, once the fourteen rivers are mentioned, then the fourteen streams, the fourteen sandy streams, the fourteen gullies, etc., can be brought into the prayer. Once the fourteen *llanos,* or plains, are mentioned, then the fourteen broad plains, the fourteen white plains, and the fourteen green plains can be mentioned. One of the practitioners tended to classify all of the features according to which of the natural phenomena they pertained to: the wind, the water, or the earth. He also classified the features based on whether or not they were associated with men's or women's activities. For example, the mountains are associated with the earth, and they are also considered masculine. Wells and pools are generally considered feminine and associated with the waters.

As a general rule, things associated with the waters are feminine and things associated with the earth masculine, although there are many exceptions. Gardens and orchards are associated with women, and cornfields with men, for they are associated with women's and men's duties, respectively. Likewise, streams and mountain rivers are associated with men because they often hunt in these places. The *encantos,* enchanted places, can be either masculine or feminine in nature. Things and places associated with the winds can be both masculine and feminine at the same time, ambisexual in nature.

At one time, I considered these classifications keys to understanding the metalanguage of dreams. They are important, but not nearly as important as the fact that the metalanguage is a projective vehicle for things better left unsaid in a small village. The major purpose of these categories is to expand the possible levels of interpretation that can be applied to a dream-tale and to provide additional levels of meaning. Narrations of dreamtime journeys are heteroglossic texts (Bakhtin 1981) that are multivocalic (Turner 1974) in nature. They have as their primary function the promotion of a fundamental dialogue between curer and client and require a dialogic interpretation.

INHABITANTS OF THE UNDERWORLD

There are basically two categories of supernatural beings who inhabit the underworld. Both classes are considered *ahmotocnihuan,* 'those who are not our brothers.' They are not part of mankind. They are distinct from the beings of the waking world on the surface of the earth and potentially dangerous to that world.

The inhabitants of the underworld in general appear much like the inhabitants of the earth's surface, though some can change their shape with great facility. For example, the lord death, *miquitagat,* can at times appear like any other villager, although perhaps a bit larger since he is a lord. At other times, he can shed his flesh and appear as a skeleton. The *miquicihuauh* can appear with the large eyes of nocturnal animals carrying huge faggots of flaming sapwood. In other situations, she can appear as any other woman would, dressed in a traditional skirt and wearing a *quechquemitl* on her headdress, which is intertwined with the hairs of all the ancestors.[14]

The inhabitants of the underworld come in two sizes. The ones called *duendes* in Spanish, the dwarfs, are slightly smaller than ordinary people in San Martín. The *taloques,* the lords and ladies of the underworld, are quite a bit larger than most villagers. Another defining characteristic of inhabitants of the underworld is whether or not they are able to leave the realms of *talocan.*

The Lesser Inhabitants of Darkness

The supernaturals that can leave the underworld to inhabit the surface of the earth *talticpac* (Knab 1978) are identified with specific natural phenomena and represent these phenomena in anthropomorphic form. They are not just the masters of these natural phenomena, but rather the phenomena themselves. For example, the *quauhtiomeh*, 'the lightning ones,' are lightning bolts personified and the *mixtimeh*, 'cloud ones,' are the anthropomorphic forms of clouds, just as the *ehecameh*, 'wind ones,' are the winds themselves.

Some of these supernaturals can inhabit the surface of the earth and are almost never found in the underworld, whereas others can be found in both places. Most of those that can be found in both regions are identified with the winds, the waters, or the earth. These are supernaturals such as the *alpixque*, 'water keepers,' the *ahuanimeh*, 'water masters,' the *ehecameh*, 'wind ones,' and the *mixtimeh*, 'cloud ones.' There are also supernaturals associated with parts of the earth not inhabited by man—the forests and uncultivated lands of the mountains—including the *tepehuane* or 'hill people' and the *mazacameh*, 'deer ones' or 'savage ones.'

All of the supernaturals who can inhabit the surface of the earth are constantly seeking souls for the underworld. This is their job on the surface of the earth. The souls they seek are those that are the easiest to capture: the souls that are out of balance with their social, natural, and supernatural environment, i.e., those that have committed some transgression against the order of the ancestors, mankind, or the natural environment. The souls they seek out are 'not of good heart,' *ahmo cualli yolotzin*. They are the souls of individuals who have not properly kept their reciprocal relationships with supernaturals of the earth or sky, with the natural environment or the social world. They are the souls of people not in harmony with their world, *ahmo cualli nehmemi*, those who 'do not live well.'

The *ahmotocnihuan*, in this sense, punish individuals who do not contribute directly to the harmonious world order. They may take their victim's hearts directly to the underworld. They may capture nothing but the dreaming *itonal*. They may send some evil wind or evil glance to inhabit the body and bring death. Or they may seek out an individual's *inagual*, either with the lord of the animals or when it wanders the surface of the earth, and cause it direct harm. It is 'those who are not our brothers,' the *ahmotocnihuan*, that cause many of the illnesses among people on the earth.

These supernaturals may in the first instance represent a kind of social control, but for most of the people of San Martín they are much more important than simply policemen of social order from *talocan*. These minions of *talocan* help maintain the harmony necessary for life on the earth.

They help to control the calamities of the natural world, the winds and the waters that can destroy life on the earth, the fruitfulness of the earth itself. They maintain the harmony of existence on the earth and can provide protection against the calamities of life as well. Offerings of flowers, candles, incense, and food can often be seen along the paths, near the pools and streams of the village. They are left for these representatives of the Most Holy Earth that share their lives with mankind.

One of the basic concepts that maintains the harmony of existence on the earth is that of reciprocity. Those who 'do not live well,' *ahmo cualli nehnemi,* and those who 'do not have good hearts,' *ahmo cualli yolotzin,* must pay for their violations of the natural order. For example, if a man has two women, a *mazacameh* or a *tepehuane* may capture one of them and eat her, or it may capture the man, his *itonal* or his *inagual,* and demand the second woman for food. Likewise, if a hunter kills too many animals, the lord of the animals, often working in concert with other supernaturals of *talocan,* will capture the hunter and hold him until he agrees to provide certain offerings and to pay for the damage he has caused to the forests and mountains.

The Lords of Darkness

There are two basic categories of supernaturals that inhabit the underworld on a permanent basis: the lords of the underworld (each with male and female counterparts) and their minions, the *taloque, talocanca, talocan-macehualli,* etc. These denizens of darkness take their orders from the lords, organizing their celebrations and doing their work.

The system in the underworld is one of patronage and labor, based on reciprocity. All the hordes of the underworld owe their lives to its lords, who protect them from the holy light, *nexti,* 'gracia' or 'grace' in Spanish. Each night, the minions of night try to capture the sun on its journey through the underworld so that they will no longer have to depend on the surface of the earth. Each year on the day before the festival of San Miguel, the hordes, enriched with harvest offerings, attempt to escape the underworld and are fought back by San Miguel and Santiago.

The lords of the underworld include the lords of the four sides of *talocan* and their female counterparts, the *ehecatagat,* the *ehecacihuat,* the *atagat,* the *acihuauh,* the *miquitagat,* etc. The *taloc* is as much a lord of the underworld as it is the embodiment of the underworld. Though there are the *señor* and *señora taloc* and the *talocan tagat* and *talocan cihuat,* all of these appear to be the same as the *taloc melauh*, with huge round eyes and "teeth like a toad."

The *talocan tagat* and the *talocan cihuat* who reside in the center of the municipal palace of *talocan*, the *presidencia* in the conceptual center of the underworld, are the same as the *señor talocan* or *señora talocan* and the *taloc melauh*, who resides in the church of the underworld under its main plaza. Sometimes all of these lords are referred to as the *presidentes de talocan*, 'presidents of the underworld,' which can be both male and female. In a certain sense, all of the lords are aspects of the *taloc*. Though the case is more difficult to make for the lords of the four sides of *talocan*, one of the practitioners did maintain that they were all the same.

The civil and religious officials of the underworld who reside in the municipal palace are for one of the practitioners more similar to the lords of the underworld, but for the other they are all definitely the *talocanca* or *taloques* who owe the lords of the underworld service and homage. The cities, towns, and villages are populated by *talocanca* and *taloques* for the most part, although all of the supernaturals can be present in the center of the underworld.

The most important of the religious officials of the underworld are the *mayordomos* of the *taloc melauh*, who arrange the great festivals of the underworld in which all the supernaturals participate. At each of the four sides of the underworld there are also festivals presided over by *mayordomos* and their assistants. There are also the armies of the underworld commanded by generals and *coroneles* who are charged with trying to capture the sun or extend the world of darkness to the surface of the earth.

At one point in a discussion of the armies of the underworld and their struggle to take over the surface of the earth or capture the sun, Doña Rubia noted that they were, in fact, rather stupid. She noted that if life on the surface of the earth perished, then there would be no one to provide sustenance for the underworld and the ancestors. They would in effect be committing suicide.

The great festivals of the underworld are basically the result of the fecundity of the surface of the earth for which the inhabitants of the underworld are responsible. The offerings left by Sanmartinos are payment for the lords of the underworld. As is sometimes said, "They don't grow anything without the light, but we don't have anything without the fruits of the Most Holy Earth." If the offerings for the lords of *talocan* are meager, they will have nothing to eat, and then they will resort to eating people. Many will die to feed the earth. *Talocan* is the ultimate consumer of life on the earth.

The Lord of the Animals

The lord of the animals, *yolcatagat,*[15] is considered the same as a lord of the underworld. The lord of the animals who keeps all the *naguals* in the underworld is unique in that he is found neither at the center of *talocan* nor at any of its four sides. The lord of the animals keeps two of each type of animal found on the surface of the earth, in the earth, in its waters, or in the air.

The lord of the animals keeps all of his animals in corrals in various places in the underworld and he only allows his animals out to help or castigate mankind on the surface of the earth. When an individual's *inagual* has been harmed, it is the lord of the animals that the curer must seek out in the underworld. If a *nagual* has been harmed, it implies that either the lord of the animals has for some reason let that animal go or that it has escaped and injured itself or perhaps has been found by a witch. The lord of the animals is always willing to help seek a lost *inagual* or resolve a problem with one of his animals.

The lord of the animals is one of the most helpful of all of the supernaturals of the underworld. Though many of the other lords of the underworld will refuse a practitioner's entreaties for aid in the underworld—perhaps due to a pact with a witch or simply because of evil intent—the lord of the animals is solely concerned with the welfare of animals and will do anything to help them. Often he will help a practitioner in battles with witches who harm his animals. The lord of the animals will also, with proper inducement such as offerings and prayers, even lend a practitioner *naguals* to help in the underworld. The practitioner can in dreams merge with these animals in addition to his or her own animal alter ego to deceive witches and malicious inhabitants of the underworld when seeking a lost or damaged soul.

SOCIAL ORGANIZATION OF THE SUPERNATURALS OF THE UNDERWORLD

Conceptually, the inhabitants of the underworld are not organized according to hierarchical classes, although in the armies of the underworld and among the officials of the underworld, there are hierarchical systems of organization like those on the surface of the earth. There is a recognized difference between full-time residents of the underworld, such as the *talo-ques* and the *talocanca,* and those denizens of darkness found in specific places. There is also a fundamental difference between the lords of darkness and their minions, the *talocanca* and *taloques* for example, as well as the other inhabitants of the underworld. The lords of darkness, the earthlords, the *talocan tagameh,* are distinct from other beings in the underworld.

The earthlords each have male and female counterparts and in a sense are ambisexual. All of the lords of the center of the underworld are considered parts of the 'true *taloc,*' which is neither male nor female. Metaphorically the earthlords of the center are called 'branches' of the 'true *taloc.*' The earthlords of the four sides of the underworld are more problematic. Though they are all considered *talocan tagameh* and *talocan cihuameh,* these are but aspects of the lords of the four sides of the underworld. Both practitioners agree that the lords of the four sides depend on the *taloc melauh* for their lives in the underworld, but only one was willing to consider them branches or parts of the earthlord. The lord of wind and the lord of death are both part of the lord of the north in the underworld. The *cuiluhuexi* or *huey ocuillin,* the earth monster of the south, is also considered a *talocan tagameh* or earthlord. The women of the west are its lords. Curiously they can be termed *talocan tagameh,* literally 'men of the underworld,' but the term is perhaps better translated as 'earthlords.' The earthlords of the east, the lords of the waters, are considered by both practitioners to be branches of the 'true *taloc.*' The lords of the east, the lords of the waters, are in fact an essential aspect of the true lord of the underworld, the earthlord, 'our mother, our father *taloc.*'

The earthlords, though they have different functions, dominate different segments of the underworld, and are ambisexual, may well be considered all parts of the earth itself. *Taloc* and *talocan* are the earth, the Most Holy Earth in all its complexity, perhaps one of the most potent parts of Mesoamerican cosmovision.

In my early attempts to classify the inhabitants of the underworld, the *ahmotocnihuan,* I based my classification almost exclusively on the residents of the underworld referred to in Spanish as *duendes,* 'dwarfs,' which can reside both in the underworld and on the surface of the earth (Knab, 1978). Including the permanent residents of the underworld in this system of classification complicates things considerably, but it does not undermine the three basic categories of underworld residents, which is based on their association with wind, water, and earth.

A modified classification begins with the *taloc melauh,* the embodiment of the underworld (see Figure 6). The earthlords of the four directions as well as those of the center can all be broken down into their primary roles with the earth, wind, and water.

The minions of the underworld obviously form a separate category from the lords. The permanent residents of the underworld must be differentiated on the basis of the social organization of the underworld, which reflects that of the surface of the earth. All of the permanent residents of the underworld are associated with the earth. They are the workers and servants of the earth and its lords, unlike the part-time residents of *talocan,* which can be associated with three phenomena dominated by the earth.

This classification of the lords and residents of the underworld reflects several important points. In terms of the social order, the differentiation of the lords, or patrons, of natural phenomena from their minions is fundamental, as is the inclusion of the winds and waters in the fundamental aspects of the earth. Many of these concepts in Mesoamerica result directly from the observation of the natural world.

Figure 6. The ahmotocnihuan: *social relationships of the inhabitants of the underworld.*

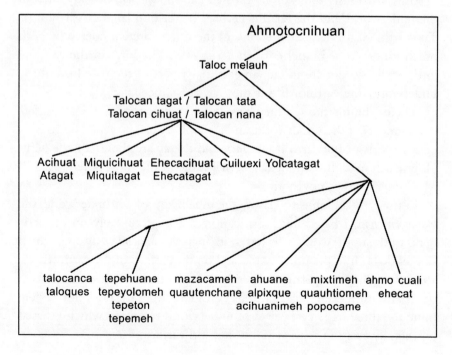

Between the underworld and the sky there is another class of supernatural which is neither *ahmotocnihuan* nor a saint of the sky. Generally
these individuals are considered as the curer's patrons. Opinions vary, but
there are between four and twelve patrons, plus the ultimate patron of
one's own teachers or lineage. Each of these patrons is associated with a
specific direction or place in the underworld. They are the curer's most
important assistants in the underworld. They are the mothers and fathers
of the 'good path,' the tradition of curing and dreaming practiced by
Rubia and Inocente that I learned. Some are leaders of messianic movements from the sixteenth and seventeenth centuries, such as Juan Ocelo,
Juan Antonio Abad, and Juan Purin. Others, such as José Antonio de la
Luz and Juan Martín de la Luz, are associated with the entryways of the
four sides of the underworld, and others, such as Juan Antonio Martín
Marqués, Manuel Antonio Francisco, and Juan Manuel Martín, are looked
on as generalized patrons of curers and keepers of the traditions of the
ancestors. These were probably well-known practitioners of this specific
tradition.

Aramoni (1990: 181) sees all of these patrons as associated with specific aspects of the underworld and specific directions. She maintains that
they sustain the underworld and actually maintain the separation of earth
and sky. Both Rubia and Inocente, however, looked on these supernaturals as powerful assistants and patrons of the tradition of curing, great
practitioners and curers, patrons of the way of the ancestors. All of them
were recognized as ancestors rather than saints (who have no ancestors).

There are also three saints considered to be specific patrons of the
curer able to inhabit both the sky and the underworld: San Juan de la Luz
Lucero de la Mañana, San Juan de los Evangelios Crecencia de Dios, and
San Miguel Protector Salvador del Mundo. Santiago Caballero is also
considered by some practitioners to be able to descend into the underworld.

CONCEPTS AND COSMOVISION: FROM NATURAL
TO SUPERNATURAL

Talocan is a concept or conceptual world based on a natural philosophy
that extends the perceived structure of the natural world into the supernatural. It is an interpretation of the unknown and unknowable from the
conscious natural world and the unconscious world of dreams.

The fundamental unity of Mesoamerica as a cultural area is based upon a conceptual unity. It is not the result of some shared laundry list of cultural traits. Even Kirchoff, who defined Mesoamerica as a cultural area (Kirchoff 1952), clearly recognized this.[16] The relationships embodied by concepts concerning the underworld of the ancestors today in San Martín Zinacapan represent a complete, coherent, and autonomous system. This is not some antiquarian fragment of the lost cityscape of Teotihuacán or Tenochtitlan. It is, instead, a geographic and conceptual system re-created throughout Mesoamerica. The same principles of the natural and supernatural worlds are true today for modern speakers of Huichol, Mazatec, Tarahumara, Otomí, and Quiché. The dialectic of observation of the natural world and traditions enculturated from birth constantly rearticulate these fundamental propositions throughout Mesoamerica.

The qualities attributed to each side of the underworld in the Sierra de Puebla are founded on a keen observation of the natural world. The north is the source of cold winds, death, and disease. East of the Plaza of San Martín it is almost possible to see the sea and to the west, mountains almost constantly shrouded in fog extend from the horizon to the highlands. In the south there are well-known hot springs near the base of Citlaltepetl, better known as the Pico de Orizaba. The conceptual nature of the supernatural world mirrors the natural world.

For villagers, some of whom have traveled extensively as traders or laborers, the features of the landscape outside the region, out of sight of the municipality of Cuetzalan, become vague and diffuse as they are in the underworld. The vast world outside the everyday experience of villagers is analogous to the vast geography of the underworld. It exists, yet it is a part of the same unconscious world that usually is occupied by dreams and fantastic tales.

The people of San Martín define their ritual landscape by what they can see from the center of their known world: the plaza of the town. These people center their world (Carrasco 1990) in a ritual landscape (Broda 1991) as Mesoamericans have for generations. The center of the underworld is a mirror of the social and political world of everyday life in San Martín.

The earthlords, the lords and ladies of the five directions, the minions of the underworld, can all in a way be seen as aspects of the earth, mirroring the types of relationships that humankind should maintain in the natural, social, and religious environment of daily life. The supernaturals of the underworld also represent fundamental natural phenomena. In fact, they are all animate embodiments of the earth, the waters, or the winds (Knab 1978). They are the models for concepts about proper social and natural relationships.

The sociology and geography of *talocan* is not arbitrary or idiosyncratic. It shows great conceptual consistency. Native practitioners are the 'natural philosophers,' the technicians of this sacred realm who must constantly analyze and expound on it in a way that is meaningful to their fellow Sanmartinos. Dreams and dreamtales articulate basic concepts about the nature and form of the underworld in a coherent and meaningful way. Journeys to the underworld of the ancestors, their explanation and interpretation, are essential for maintaining the human soul in a harmonious balance with the natural and supernatural environments. This balance is essential for the maintenance of life on the earth, just as the fruits of the earth—corn, beans, squash, etc.—are essential for sustenance.

Practitioners must make their explanation and interpretation of the underworld of the ancestors coherent with traditions of the natural and social environment for them to be meaningful for villagers. The essential feature of the metalanguage of dreams and dreams themselves is that they explain tenuous experiences in the world of darkness, *talocan,* in a coherent and meaningful way. The practitioner's first formulation of a dream narrative allows the client, his or her family, and other participants to speculate on the nature of the unknown from the known world of experience. Within the framework of a shared conceptual system, participants can speculate on the nature of the unconscious and unknown world of *talocan* based on the known world of everyday life.

In restoring the soul to its necessary harmonious balance with the natural, social, and supernatural worlds in this way, the practitioner reaffirms fundamental concepts, values, and relationships. In order to cure, he or she brings to bear on the problems of everyday life all of the traditions of the natural, social, and supernatural worlds. Dreams of life in the Most Holy Earth are for the people who live on the earth.

CHAPTER FIVE

DREAMS AND CURING

The Dialogics of Curing

DREAM ANALYSIS IN THE SIERRA DE PUEBLA does not follow Freud's technique of analyzing the client's dreams, but rather uses dreams as an open-ended vehicle for interpretation, a kind of a Rorschach test in words. As shown in Chapter 2, the dream is transformed as it is told to and interpreted for the client. The practitioner fashions dreamtime experience on the basis of his or her knowledge of the traditions of the ancestors and the client's situation into a tale of journeys in the supernatural world of *talocan*. The dreamtale itself is but a metalanguage that is the basis for dialogue. It is the dialogue of curer, client, family, and friends with the traditions of the ancestors and everyday life that is of interest here.

The dreamtale as a metalanguage is as Bakhtin (1986: 136) has observed: "not simply a code, it always has a dialogical relationship to the language it describes and analyzes." The language of the discourse of dreams that cure is the language of the tradition of the ancestors and *talocan,* which, as we have seen in Chapter 4, has a distinctive structure and set of rules. The dreamtale provokes a therapeutic dialogue and as Bakhtin (Todorov 1984: 31) observed about Freudianism: "What is related in these utterances is not the dynamics of the individual soul, but the *social dynamics* of the

interrelations of doctor and patient."What emerges in the dialogue of curing is the curer, client, family, and friends puzzling out the meaning of the
dreamtale in social, symbolic, political, and religious terms. The traditions
of the ancestors are thus relevant to their everyday lives.

The metalanguage of dreams is no more unusual than the metalanguage of Freudian analysis, literary criticism, or Marxist sociology. The
form, structure, and even geography of the underworld are the essential
tools for expressing the maladies of the human soul. As Bakhtin has also
observed (Todorov 1984: 18): "The spirit, mine as well as the other's, is
not given, like a thing (like the immediate object of the natural sciences);
rather it comes through the expression in signs, a realization through 'texts,'
which is of equal value to the self and to the other." What emerges from
the conceptual geography of the unknown is essentially the role of the
human spirit in everyday life. This is the dialogical basis for curing the
human soul in the Sierra de Puebla.

Looking at the dream and the dreamtale as a process for interpretation,
rather than an object of interpretation as in the Western tradition, is fundamental to understanding this system. The mythopoetic function of
dreams has long been recognized in psychiatry from what Carl Jung
(1916) called the "active imagination" to "guided imagery" therapies
(Price-Williams 1987: 247). But as Bakhtin (1981: 276) has observed of
the dialogic process: "The living utterance having taken meaning and
shape at a particular historic moment in a socially specific context cannot
fail to brush up against thousands of living dialogical threads woven in
the socio-ideological constructions around the given object of an utterance, it cannot fail to become an active participant in the social dialogue."
As an active part of the social dialogue of curing, the mythopoetic dreamtale constitutes a heteroglossic text that is open to a multiplicity of dialogical threads of meaning. The interpretation and reinterpretation of
dreams serves as the basis for the therapeutic dialogue in the social world.

In this type of analysis, the significance of the method is not to be
found in the dreams themselves, but rather in the fact that they serve as a
basis for communication, an open-ended interpretation of the events of
everyday life. In the curing process, prayers are the templates against which
knowledge is compared (see Chapter 3). The ritual and offerings define
the socio-ideological context for the dialogic interaction (see Chapter 2),
and the dreamtale is the heteroglossic text to be speculated upon and
interpreted.

DREAMTALES AND THE DIALOGIC PROCESS

In the dialogic process of curing, the metaphoric search for maladies of the human spirit links together in a concrete way cosmological concepts of the underworld and everyday life. The underworld of the ancestors is a nebulous and largely indeterminate world unlike the natural world on which it is modeled. This is essential in understanding the flexibility in interpreting dreams and the underworld.

The metalanguage of dreams permits the practitioner to accommodate the interpretation of a dream to the context of the client, the client's family, and the village, using the places of indeterminate location in the underworld as a vehicle in fashioning the dreamtale. In this system, it is difficult if not impossible to present a simple laundry list of symbols or motifs, each with their appropriate interpretation and meaning in the underworld. Meanings change according to the context of the journey in the underworld, the client, the client's family and relatives. Meanings also change according to the level of interpretation, whether the client is male or female, young or old.

The heteroglossic text (Todorov 1984: 56–59) of the dreamtale is a metalanguage that forms the basis for dialogic interpretation. The text itself can be constituted in a multiplicity of ways. It is never a fixed text, but rather a fluid dialogue of tradition, the underworld of the ancestors in the natural world of everyday life. There are in fact many ways that dream experience can be expressed as a dreamtale (see Chapter 2). The symbols and motifs of the dreamtale are of secondary importance to the dialogical process that emerges from interpretation.

The metalanguage of dreams is so fluid and packed with the meanings of tradition that hearers of virtually the same dream text can arrive at vastly different interpretations. Even the practitioner can modify the dreamtale in each telling (see Chapter 2). Interpretation, not just of the metalanguage of dreams but of the underworld itself, is therefore essentially dialogical in nature, an endless series of dialogues interpreting the traditions, metaphors, meanings, and concepts of the ancestors and *talocan*. As Bakhtin (1981: 282) noted: "In the actual life of speech, every concrete act of understanding is active. It assimilates the word to be understood into its own conceptual system."

When a practitioner analyzes the dreams of others, the first act is to transform the telling of the dream into a journey to the underworld. Once the dream has been transformed, its true nature elucidated by the practitioner as a series of events on the earth and in the earth, it is open for interpretation. The first dialogue of interpretation is the transformation of the dream to a metalanguage: the metaphoric journey to the underworld. The second dialogue is the interpretation of the transformed dream by the curer, the client, the anthropologist, or the reader. Dreams are seen as having meanings hidden within them, as in the obscurity and mist of the underworld, which are brought to light through interpretation.

A good example of this is the sixteenth dream of my own training as a practitioner. The version that I kept in notes and the version that I told in Nahuat are superficially different, yet I sought to put the dream in terms that both native practitioners would understand. I converted it into the metalanguage in the dreamtale.

The dream as kept in notes was as follows:

I was taken down a long tunnel of bright colors. I could not move but was swept along. There was a sixteenth-century Spanish courtyard with arches all around it, and in the center a stone fountain of rose-colored stone spouting bright blue, not white, waters. There was a small man standing next to the fountain in *calzones,* white indigenous clothes, who was speaking in an animated way and signaling me to come near. I could hear nothing. Then there were voices, shouts and screams in Spanish: "Get out!" "Move!" "Get away!" The galleries under the arches were filled with people shouting. Their faces were horrible, like masks that moved, and they were all coming closer and shouting.

The man, who looked a lot like Inocente, though I couldn't really see his face, motioned to me. He grabbed at me as I came closer. His arms were short like a dwarf's, and there were great protrusions from his body that stabbed me. He grabbed me and pulled me there into the blue water, holding on to me and taking me by the head in his small arms.

"Come here!" he said in Nahuat.

There was a long passage and I could feel myself walking in a dark place. The man grasped my face with his little arms, and the protrusions of his body were hurting me so I wrenched myself free.

There was a light and a face in the light like old Rubia, an old woman in white. Everything there was white and light, and then it all turned dark and there was one horrific face with huge teeth salivating. It would eat me! And then I saw nothing.

From there I came out of a great dark place into a coffee plantation where there were people in indigenous dress seated and talking and women weaving. It was green, as green as spring, and I wanted to walk but I couldn't. I felt like I was bound, and everyone came around to look at me and laugh.

There was such an uproar that I awoke.

In the actual telling, this dream was transformed into something I thought Rubia and Inocente could better understand. At this point, both Rubia and Inocente had been telling me dreams for quite some time, I had been to innumerable curings, and I had already begun the process of initiation and learning to cure with dreams. I knew what events were expected in dreams, and I was learning to transform them into metaphoric journeys to the underworld.

The dream that I recounted in Nahuat was as follows:

I was in a deep river, and I was dragged along. It was in the forest, in the mountains, where I saw bright greens and flowers of many colors that I passed.

When I came out of the river, I was in a patio with walls all around me where there were people. They were all screaming at me to get out of there. In the center of the patio was a well that was the color of the sky and there was a man near the well who beckoned me to come to him.

At this point it was impolite to say that the man looked like Inocente. This could have been him in the dream, but I didn't want to say that I had seen him in the dream, for he would then be vulnerable to my having taken his soul in the next section of the dream.

The man was a dwarf, one of those things from the cave, and he grabbed me with his little hands on the face, by the head. I fought with him, and he took me there into the water, into the well there. There were people there in the patio, but none of them helped; they laughed and yelled at me to leave.

"Come here!" the little man shouted. The dwarf took me down into the well, holding on to me with his little arms.

He took me by the hands and motioned me to come with him. I followed along a long dark path with the little man holding on to me. I ran away and got myself free of that dwarf, and there was the *tlacuache* who took me to another place.

The *tlacuache,* or possum, here is the *nonagual* that is used for getting from one place to another in the underworld. I chose this to indicate that I was not certain in this dream how I got from one place to another.

There was an old woman there dressed in *naguas.*[1] As I came closer to her, she changed. She had a huge mouth and she was going to eat me; there were flames and there was smoke there and there was the gnashing of teeth there. Chomp! Chomp, Chomp! Chomp! She was going to eat me there in that place with huge teeth I could see.

I don't know if I got away, but then I was in a coffee plantation where there were people. It was green and it was bright. Maybe it was the paradise, the one that has been talked about, foretold. I couldn't move there; I was bound.

Then they all came out to look at me, and they were laughing and talking. They had big teeth and they were not our brothers. I couldn't move, and then I saw the *tlacuache*. It helped me there, it gnawed through the thongs that bound me, and I went with it. I was with it and then I got out of there.

This dream was quite different than most. It was the final dream in my training in which both practitioners concurred that I had found the center of the underworld. This was what Paul Friedrich (Attinasi and Friedrich 1995: 37–40) would call a dialogical breakthrough in fieldwork. By this time I had already learned from the analysis of previous dreams to transform the experiences of the dream into events that were understandable for both practitioners in terms of the metalanguage of dreams and to construct a dreamtale that would form the dialogical basis for further interpretation.

The initial feeling of traveling down a long tunnel was interpreted as flowing down a stream because I did not at that point feel as if I was walking but rather being drawn. I illustrated the feeling of colors by mentioning leaves and flowers that grow along the banks of a stream in accordance with the interpretation of flowing in the water.

I illustrated the fountain as a well like the one near the center of town and the sixteenth-century patio as simply a patio in order to simplify the description of places that the practitioners had never seen. Although in my actual dream it was clearly an ornate colonial building with arches and an elegant carved fountain, this simplification was necessary to avoid lengthy explanation. In retrospect, the representation of an ancient build- ing and fountain in simplified terms allowed both curers to see this as the central patio of the underworld, much like the plaza of the town. The simplification allowed for greater interpretation, which is more highly valued in dreamtales. The practitioners interpreted the people around the patio as the minions of the underworld who were trying to prevent me from entering its very heart.

Both practitioners agreed that the little man must have been an under- world lord, and I did not disabuse them of this by mentioning that it looked like Inocente. They interpreted this as the man taking me for food to the true lord of the underworld, the *taloc melauh.* My escape from the man meant that I would not be consumed. The lords look like ordinary people, they explained, and they are transformed as one nears them. In this part of the dream, I felt as if I was actually walking and used the stan- dard interpretation of being on a path, a powerful metaphor in Nahuat.

The *tlacuache,* or possum, motif was fortuitous.[2] I had noticed that when events in their own dreamtales did not seem connected, both practition- ers used an animal as the link that took them from one place to another. As I later learned, these animal aspects of the soul are intimately involved with witchcraft and are acquired assistants in the world of dreams. As the curer becomes more adept, he or she acquires additional animals, which are a part of the practitioner's soul and assistants in the underworld. With each additional animal, the practitioner acquires personality traits of the animal and a body of ritual knowledge about the animal including some very effective techniques of witchcraft.

These techniques are part of the body of secret knowledge passed from one practitioner to another and almost never discussed. My use of the possum, *tlacuache,* in this dream began a long and complicated discussion of the traits of animals and people and how one discovers one's own ani- mal alter ego in dreams. Finding the nature of one's own animal coun- terpart is essential in becoming a practitioner, and acquiring additional animal assistants is essential in learning the techniques of the tradition. It also embodies a great deal of knowledge of the techniques of witchcraft.

Of the three basic ways individuals are recruited into the tradition of curing, the first, through severe magical maladies such as magical fright, *susto,* or *nemouhtil,* which requires the initiate to search for his or her own lost soul, is the most common. In order to search for his or her soul, the individual must apprentice himself or herself to a practitioner and learn the tradition. This is how I was recruited to the tradition (Knab 1995). The second method of recruitment is hereditary, where the practitioner will request a member of his or her own family to take on the tradition, usually because of a repeated dream. The third method of recruitment is by divine intervention. Individuals who survive lightning strikes, snakebites, severe wounds in battle, or ambushes are usually obliged to seek out a practitioner and learn the tradition. Today many people recruited to the tradition do not take on the full burden and thus never learn to construct the dreamtale or manipulate animal alter egos. This is sometimes due to a lack of financial means to obtain the offerings necessary, but in some cases it is out of fear of being associated with witchcraft.

It is obligatory for practitioners to train at least one individual in the tradition before they die or their souls will forever wander in the underworld. The process of initiation into the tradition can take years, and the process of mastering it is a lifelong endeavor. Taking on this tradition is viewed as a lifelong obligation of service to the Most Holy Earth and the villagers of San Martín. It begins with learning to dream and to tell a proper dreamtale.

TRANSFORMING THE DREAM: THE DREAMTALE

The metalanguage of dreams borrows freely from all sources of knowledge of the underworld. In the above example, I transformed the dream into a journey to the underworld. I was beginning to understand how the dreamtale is constructed out of the dream event, the conventional descriptions for specific types of dream experience, and the motifs that are an acceptable part of the dreamtale. The practitioners had already described most of the important points in the underworld to me in extensive analyses of my own dreams. Thus, using my knowledge of the underworld, the metalanguage of dreams, conventional ways of describing dream experience that I had learned, and motifs widely used in dreamtales, I constructed an acceptable dreamtale.

Perhaps the most important point about the metalanguage of dreams is to be found in the discourse of dreams. On the basis of an intimate knowledge of the underworld, the form and structure of *talocan,* native practitioners reconstruct the content of dreams, which are vague recollections of obscure events for clients. Taking into account the structure of the underworld, the earth and the sky, and the commonsense knowledge of the events of everyday life, practitioners can establish a dialogue with clients based on the dreamtale couched in the world of dreams that is a coherent vehicle of communication. As Bakhtin (Todorov 1984: 30) notes: "No utterance in general can be attributed to the speaker exclusively; *it is the product of interaction of interlocutors,* and, broadly speaking of the whole complex *social situation* in which it has occurred." The dreamtale thus becomes a coherent vehicle for interpretation and communication among all participants in a curing ritual.

Certain features are essential to understanding the underworld, *talocan,* in dreams. First, the form and structure of the underworld reflect the conceptual divisions of everyday life in the village. Though there are some inversions, the two worlds are analogous. Second, the form and structure of the underworld are defined by the existence of certain fixed points with a specific content but varying interpretations. The points chosen are those that afford maximal interpretation through dialogue. Third, context can modify meaning. Both the internal context of events within a dream and the context within which the dream is recounted can modify meaning. That is why flexible, nebulous, often obscure places and events are necessary. Fourth, given that there are distinct levels of interpretation and explanation, each dream may be subject to various interpretations. The most correct interpretation is that arrived at through a dialogue based on the dream text. The dream text may be constituted in various ways to promote that dialogue. The greater the potential for interpretation, the more highly valued the dreamtale.

The underworld has a geography that coherently reflects the conceptual divisions of space in everyday life (see Chapter 4). Each distinct location in the underworld has a symbolic content that is reflected in and interpreted through the events of everyday life. Each place in the underworld has a specific and distinctive meaning, but events can alter these meanings according to the context of the dream or the client's situation.

The basic structure of the dreamtale is dictated by the content of distinct locations in the underworld. In general this structure follows commonly held concepts of everyday life in the village. It is an adequate yet indirect means of communication concerning the events of everyday life.

This indirect manner of communication between curer and client is essential. It permits the participants to maintain an indirect dialogue in terms of events in the underworld that accurately reflects the occurrences of everyday life in the village, which may be at the root of a client's problems.

There are two fundamental steps in dream interpretation that can perhaps best be illustrated by an example of a curer analyzing the dream of someone other than herself. The first act is to transform the dream into a journey into the underworld using the metalanguage of dreams to fashion the dreamtale. This is the same thing that the practitioner does when metaphorically "bearing the dream into the light," or converting it into a dreamtale in the proper metalanguage. The second step in the process is the interpretation of the dream. In this particular case, there were several interpretations of the dream, none of which was judged by participants as particularly important, yet the interpretative dialogue proved crucial in finding a cure for the client.

The client in this case was a girl, Luz, of about nine or ten years, who had become listless and unable to sleep and refused to eat. This was the third time that Rubia had tried to find a cause for the girl's condition, and at this point she had already recounted one dream with little discussion or interpretation. She asked if anyone had perhaps seen the girl in their dreams or if there was anything that someone had seen in the underworld that might help her to search out the girl's soul. She was by this point convinced that this was a case of soul loss, *susto,* or *nemtouhil,* but had no idea of its cause.

The girl's mother, Remedios, volunteered that she had a dream, which she recounted as follows:

> I was carrying a big bundle of cornstalks up the hill on a wide stone path, and when I arrived at the top of the mountain everything was green and growing again, even the cornstalks that I was carrying. They were all filled with fresh new corn, and they were very heavy.
>
> There was a little dirt path there which I followed to a house near the top of the mountain, and there I set the bundle down.

There was no one home and I sat down to wait. When I turned around, the bundle was gone and I went to look for it.

There were two men in the cornfield as I went back to the *camino real,* the royal or great path, but when I went to them they disappeared and I had to climb back up the mountain. When I got to the *camino real,* the two men were on the path ahead of me and I went after them but they disappeared again. I kept on walking down the *camino real* a long, long way, but I couldn't see the men. They were gone and so was all of that beautiful corn.

Rubia's first comment on this was that the men were *tepeyolomeh,* the hill heart people. She then proceeded to retell the dream as follows:

You were walking up one of the hills there (in *talocan*) and that's where the hill heart ones live. They have their houses there on the tops of the hills there. It's an enchanted place where everything grows, there where they live. That's why your cornstalks were green and full of corn.

They're the ones who make everything grow there, but it's all theirs. They took those big green ears of corn from you there. You should have kept them on your back! It was surely their house you found there on the top of the mountain, and you're lucky they were satisfied with the corn and didn't eat you too. They would have, you know. When you go off on those little paths, that's where they get you.

When you looked for them, they were probably going to try to trick you, get you off into the forest or into a deep pit. They were just waiting for you to go after them. Then you'd really be a goner. You were lucky you went back to the *camino real.*

They were still out to get you on the *camino real* but you were lucky they didn't get you off of it again. You went a long, long way on the *camino* and they didn't get you. Well, that's good. Maybe they were happy with their corn. You see, they didn't steal your corn— you took their corn.

Rubia was already interpreting in her retelling of the dreamtale. Her first interpretation was that maybe Remedios had angered the hill heart ones and they had taken her daughter's soul. Her husband thought that maybe Remedios should have stayed on the path, and Rubia agreed. Rubia then started talking about how dangerous it was to stray off the path[3] and asked if Luz knew enough to stay on the path when they went places, suggesting that perhaps the girl had fallen off the path and lost her soul. The parents both said that she always stayed nearby and that she hadn't fallen that they knew of. The path in this case is a powerful metaphor for the road of life and the proper way things should be done.

Rubia then suggested that perhaps the *tepeyolomeh* were still angry, but Remedios said that she had only had this dream after her daughter had become ill. Remedios thought that maybe the hill heart ones already had little Luz's *itonal* and that was why her cornstalks sprouted "children," the ears of corn.

Miguel, Luz's father, thought that the path was what this dream was all about, and that one had to remain on a "good path," *camino real,* or suffer harm. Rubia agreed with him and commented that it had been dangerous for his wife to set down her bundle near the house of the *tepeyolomeh,* off of the path. This broke down into a rather metaphoric discussion of living a "good life," *cualli nehnemi,* and staying on a "good path," with everyone agreeing that the "good path" was the way things should be done.

The dream was inconclusive, and Rubia agreed to try again to find the child's lost soul. The child, who was present for all of this, had heard a long discussion of what it was to live a good life and seen considerable concern for her well-being on the part of her elders. Though this didn't cure her, it may have helped.

Rubia was of the opinion that perhaps Remedios was right and the *tepeyolomeh* had Luz's soul. Her next dream was a rather dramatic account of a confrontation with the *tepeyolomeh* in *talocan,* but she failed to locate the child's lost soul. She then suggested that offerings be taken up to a nearby mountaintop by a group of relatives. By this time the girl was already quite a bit better and it may have been due in no small part to the collective concern for her on the part of her elders. In her final dream, Rubia found the girl's lost soul and freed it by using the offerings her family had left on the mountaintop.

The interpretative dialogue in this case was crucial in marshalling the concern of Luz's elders, showing her the basic moral lessons of the traditions of the ancestors, and eventually locating her lost soul. At each stage in the process of this curing, the dream event was first transformed into a dreamtale that provided a broad basis for the interpretative dialogue and involved many individuals in the dialogical process of finding the girl's lost soul.

INTERPRETING AN INTERPRETATION

The interpretation of dreams—whether they be the dreams of curers or anyone else—is an important matter in San Martín (see Chapter 2). The dreams themselves are not nearly as important in everyday life as their interpretation and reinterpretation. The constant discussion of dreams allows people to map, project, modify, and extend their perception of the known and the unknown into the actions of everyday life (see Ricoeur 1970).

In Western traditions, this has similarities with Jung's (1916) active imagination, allowing the experience to unfold, enrich, and inform the unconscious. It is a process of conjecture that extends into the collective activities of everyday life. Gaston Bachelard's cosmic reverie brings the notion of the hyper-real or supernatural together with the real. For as he states, "One has never seen the world well unless he has dreamed what he was seen in it" (Bachelard 1969: 173). For Sanmartinos, the experience of the dream merges the known and the unknown, the natural and super- natural, the conscious and unconscious. The problem is to interpret this in everyday life. As shown in the previous example, the real value of the dreamtale comes from the process of its interpretation.

Dreams are not just manifestations of unconscious drives and desires, and the wayward soul is not simply a metaphor for the unconscious in San Martín. Conscious and unconscious motives are constantly part of the discussion of dreams. As Gilbert Herdt (1987: 81) has pointed out, in soci- eties that view dreams as reality there is a cultural problem with Freud's notions of the separateness of consciousness.

The language of reporting dreams constitutes the metalanguage of dreams. Ricoeur (1976: 58) has observed that Freud never understood that the symbolic nature of dreams was based on the language and cul- ture of their manifestations. The metalanguage of dreams used in the Sierra de Puebla is a highly codified system based on a coherent Mesoamerican cosmovision and natural philosophy that merges conscious and uncon- scious, natural and supernatural.

Dreams are not just private manifestations of an inner unconscious world. They are tales of the wandering soul that are public domain, part of public discourse. Dreams provide a wide range of interpretative possibilities on the basis of traditional views. The wider the interpretative possibilities of a particular dream, the greater its value and the more likely it is to become a part of public discourse and gossip.

This is not to deny that dreams have deep personal and unconscious components. There are personal aspects of dreams, such as the beings encountered in them, which are rarely or never mentioned. Here it must also be pointed out that this elimination of the personal from the dream allows a far wider range of possible interpretations. Thus, it implies a greater value.

A short example of a woman's fear of being violated by a particular in-law was told to me in private by Rubia and then incorporated into her own dreamtale recounted in the process of curing the woman's sister. Rubia recounted the following dream with her usual wry commentary:

> Well, she told me that she was walking along the path near the orchards up the mountain. She shouldn't go up there alone anyway, and I hope that she doesn't really do that, because if she does she's really up to no good. There were big fruits on the trees there and they were ripe, falling on the ground. Some of them were even partly eaten she said.[4]
>
> Well, she was a big juicy fruit waiting to be eaten too, but she didn't know it yet. She picked off some of the fruit and put it in her *huacal,* basket. She took a stick to shake some of the fruit down and out came Don Pedro, her brother-in-law, and he was ready for her with his stick there alright, the big ugly thing [his penis].
>
> Well, "No," she said, "get it away from here!" But he came after her and he sure had a good taste of that ripe fruit of hers. He held her and he had her and then she ran through the forest, through the mountain back to her house where she awoke.

When Rubia told me this dream, even she noted that it was unusual for the woman to mention her brother-in-law by name. She wasn't certain whether this was out of fear of Don Pedro or revenge. Perhaps the young woman hoped that Rubia, knowing where to find Don Pedro's soul at the orchard in dreams, could prevent him from finding her. Maybe she even hoped that Rubia could arrange for something a bit bad to happen to him via witchcraft.

Whatever the woman's motivation for telling Rubia the details of this dream, she was expressing a very direct, personal fear. Whether it was a portent of things to come or something that had already happened, Rubia was not sure. Rubia's solution to the problem was to tell the woman not to go out alone and to avoid the orchards.[5]

The same dream came up in a curing for the woman's sister a few days later, and there were various interpretations offered for it. The dream was as follows:

> Well, then I was going up on one of the great highways to the top of the mountain, and there was a great green orchard filled with big ripe fruits, all of them at the same time,[6] apples and guavas and peaches. There were many of them on the ground and there were some that had been eaten. They were all ripe and juicy.
>
> I was reaching up for them so very high. With a stick I got some of them, standing up so high, and I put them into my basket.
>
> Then I saw him, one of those things, one of them! A *talocan hacendado,* with his big ugly thing [penis] pointed out at me there. Those *hacendados* have the biggest sticks [penises], taller than most men. They can kill with them, and they'll get anyone. They don't care who they get.[7]
>
> He was after some fresh ripe fruit alright. So, I threw all of the fruit at him and I ran out of there back down the mountain and away from the orchard until I came to a stream.

The young woman's father commented on this part, specifically saying that no woman should go out to the orchards alone. The *hacendados,* hacienda owners, who are the prototypical rapists of the underworld, would get them and split them apart there. Her mother commented that her husband was right, but the *hacendados* would get anyone who took their fruit. To taste a juicy fruit is a metaphor for having sexual intercourse, and the *hacendados* are known as being desirous of sexual intercourse with anyone. This brought on a discussion of "tasting the fruit" that focused on both proper and improper relations, their consequences, their prevalence in town, and the question of rape, whether or not a woman could resist someone's advances without falling seriously ill or losing her soul to fear.

Rape was in this case considered a possible reason for soul loss, and any kind of illicit sexual activity was an invitation to the supernaturals of the underworld to consume the perpetrators. Men could resist being caught by the supernaturals of the underworld more than women, Rubia commented, but eventually the earth ate them too.

Interpretive Dialogue

As a personal dream, this particular dream expresses unconscious fears of one individual. When it was transformed into the metalanguage of dreams to an event in the underworld, it became a broad, general, and meaningful vehicle of discussion for sexual themes that are very highly repressed in the Nahua world. The metalanguage confers on dreams the mythopoetic, cosmological, and philosophical dimensions that transform them into a broad tapestry for discussing events of everyday life in terms of traditional values.

THE CLIENT

For the client, a practitioner's dream may or may not have a direct and personal meaning. Since the practitioner is fundamentally working to restore the client's soul to its proper position in the world, the practitioner strives to tell a dreamtale that will have value and relevance for the client. The practitioner must make the dream understandable for the client. Too much of his or her esoteric knowledge or personal experience in the world of dreams would not be understandable for the client. In his or her initial discussions with the client and the client's family and friends, and in the initial prayers and offerings, the practitioner seeks to establish a framework for the dreams that will follow and their discussion.

This framework is laid with the types of offerings requested. Some may be hot: copal incense, candles, tobacco, and *aguardiente*. Some may be cold: flowers, leaves, water, corn, beans, or tortillas. These offerings may also indicate where the practitioner suspects the client's problem to be located in the underworld. Most people know that the north is cold and thus requires more hot offerings, whereas the south is hot and requires cold things. There are the waters of the east, which require foods from dry land, and there are the mountains in the west that require things from the lowlands. If the practitioner suspects that particular supernaturals of the underworld are involved, there will be specific offerings for them. The *alpixque,* for example, have a particular liking for certain flowers, and the *mazacameh* particularly like tender, young, sweet grasses. Practitioners will explain in detail what offerings are needed and why they are needed. This is an essential part of the framework for curing the soul.

The curer will also modify prayers to specific situations, emphasizing specific sections and even saying them in a particularly loud and irreverent voice. And when prayers are finished, a practitioner will often even explain to the client, family, and friends why and where specific things are in the underworld in order to assure a proper framework for the dreams that he or she seeks.

Specific places in the underworld that are visited in dreams have specific symbolic implications. Some come from everyday life, such as places for men's and women's activities. Men hunt along streams and in the forest while women wash at broad streams and congregate at wells (at least they did before there was running water in the village). Men clear and plant cornfields, and women harvest corn and coffee. There are cold places in the shadows of mountains and hot places where there are secluded glades and warm stream banks. There are good and bad roads and paths. There are dangerous parts of the uninhabited forests, and there are safe, small houses and lean-tos scattered throughout the underworld as they are on the surface of the earth. Each has certain symbolic implications. In this particular dream, the client heard her sister's dream transformed into a general event in the underworld, which made it a good vehicle for the dialogic interpretation of sexual fears.

There are also the enchanted places from narrative and tradition in the underworld, such as hill heart shrines, cave mouths, waterfalls, and large deep pools. These places, though never actually seen, are known, and they have specific symbolic implications. Practitioners have a repertoire of places with specific symbolic implications that is far more extensive than the repertoires of most villagers.

Early in my own training, I was under the impression that the particular symbolic content of a place in the underworld made the metalanguage an indirect means of signaling the events of everyday life. For trained practitioners this is often the case, but most villagers do not share completely this esoteric knowledge. Practitioners in most cases must explain such things to their clients and their client's families and friends. The specific symbolic content of places in the world of dreams is in fact manifested almost exclusively in a pragmatic manner. It is explained where necessary to promote discussion and interpretation of dreams.

THE FAMILY

Although practitioners do have an extensive notion of the esoteric meanings of each place visited in the world of dreams, one quickly recognizes by the blank stares on one's clients, faces that all but the most transparent of these are in fact the practitioner's exclusive domain for esoteric discussions of their tradition. The symbolic content of the many places of dreamtime travels make one suspect that there is a simple laundry list or cookbook approach to interpreting dreams and dream motifs, but this is not the case. Even practitioners do not consistently agree. Interpretation is the result of a polyphonous dialogue concerning a heteroglossic text. This is where the client's family and friends come in, through the multiple interpretations that they offer.

The interpretation of dreams is essentially a pragmatic activity merging the known with the unknown and the natural with the supernatural. The meanings that result from dreams are to be found in the act of interpretation and discussion led by practitioners and participated in by all.

The pragmatic nature of interpretation does not mean that it is little more than a therapeutic gossip session. It is based on a tradition and a fundamental Mesoamerican cosmovision that codifies the relationship of mankind to the world at large. The metalanguage of dreams places events that are specifically adapted to the client's needs firmly in a context of tradition: traditional values and morals; traditional social and geographical divisions; traditional notions of health, sickness, and death. In this last case, even the motifs from the client's sister's dream proved highly productive in the dialogic process.

The practitioner's role is to sift through the multiple interpretations, speculations, and conjectures of all participants and find those that show how or where the client may have become metaphorically out of balance with the social or natural world of tradition. The practitioner may dream many times and sift through hundreds of interpretations in the process.

INTERPRETING THE CAUSES OF CONFLICTS

The causes of imbalances of the soul and its disequilibrium in the world of everyday life are as varied as each individual. It may be the result of conflicts among family members, a lost love, guilt over the transgression of certain moral precepts, fear of a particular individual, or any of a thousand other causes. The practitioner must find a way of describing it in terms of the traditional notions of the soul and a limited number of types of possible dislocations of the human soul (see Chapter 1).

The three fundamental aspects of the soul are each a different locus of life on the earth. The *iyollo* is the internal animic force, which can be inhabited, or pushed out of the body, the central locus of life and the cosmos. An evil wind, an evil glance, or witchcraft can do damage to the human body just as a slash or a wound can. A person can be damaged by envy, spite, vicious intention on the part of others, or witchcraft, which will effect the *iyollo*.

The *itonal* is a more ephemeral aspect of the soul. It can be taken away, captured, scared out of the body, or simply lost. The lost *itonal* wanders the world alone until it is found or its owner dies. The captured *itonal* is forcibly held in darkness by someone's evil intent toward the individual or by the lords of the underworld for some transgression against tradition. This kind of imbalance is retribution for some act that must be discovered to bring the soul back. Magical fright, unintentional soul loss, results from a lack of attention to the acts of everyday life. The lost soul must be found to restore harmony to the individual. The individual must be made conscious of his or her acts in everyday life to discover and keep this aspect of the soul.

Damage to an *inagual* can be simply accidental. In such a case, it may have escaped from the care of the lord of the animals, indicating an evil or wild intention on the part of the individual. The *inagual,* which is intimately involved with witchcraft, can be harmed by a witch or do battle with a witch. This wild and sinister aspect of the personality is cold and dark. It is that aspect of a person that is most likely to harm other individuals. It may in turn be harmed, either by provoking a witch or by simply escaping the care of the lord of the animals. It is the lord of the animals' role in the world of tradition to see that these wild and savage aspects of personality do not harm each other and are not harmed by others.

When a client is diagnosed with a disease of the soul, this implies a fundamental discord or disharmony of the soul with its environment. There are possibly as many ways to restore the soul as there are reasons for discord, and each depends on the particular client and his or her family and friends for resolution. Some types of dissonance are resolved merely by dreaming and discussing the dreams. Interpretation, concern, and attention to a person's soul can often restore it.

In the case of inhabitations, the patient may be massaged and pulsed to find the source of the problem, which is ritually removed. The removal of objects that have inhabited an individual is a metaphoric cleansing. Both the client and curer know that this is not the actual removal of a tooth or feather, but that the object ritually removed is a metaphor for a fundamental problem of the soul. Practitioners are not charlatans using slight of hand to pull objects from a client's body. They are in fact ritually removing objects that represent real, albeit metaphoric, inhabitations of the soul. Ritual teas and sweat baths, combined with compassionate concern for the client, restore balance to the soul.

The conflicts of everyday life are not always conscious, but rather hidden from view and glossed over by seemingly normal patterns of behavior. Conflicts nevertheless exist. These conflicts are often at the root of imbalances of the human soul. It is the practitioner's task to ascertain what these conflicts are. This is done by talking to people, gossiping, dreaming and interpreting dreams, projecting on and speculating on the possible causes for a soul's discord with the traditional order of things. Once the practitioner has a solid notion of the basic problems of a client, a diagnosis is offered in terms of the basic relation of the soul to its environment.

Diagnosis is only a single step toward resolution. The conflicts that underlie the disequilibrium must then be resolved. Ritual is the practitioner's primary tool in effecting a resolution and restoration of the soul. There are two distinctive types of ritual resolution that are common for problems of the soul. Symbolic resolution of a client's problems sounds like sympathetic magic, but it is in fact far more effective. Manipulating a commonly held symbol system provides the client a means of dealing with, at least on a metaphoric level, the sources of conflict.

The second method of ritual resolution is manipulation of the social system to eliminate conflict. Individuals with whom a client has a conflict, or whose conflict may be causing the client's problems, may be asked to participate in rituals that bind them together in socially prescribed patterns of behavior. They may be asked to make offerings together or to perform ceremonies that bind them as ritual kin. They may be asked to participate in a ritual pilgrimage or to assist the client in some arduous task required to restore his or her soul to balance. All of these ritual prescriptions require that participants resolve imbalances in the soul according to tradition.

RITUAL AS CONFLICT RESOLUTION

There are rituals that symbolically resolve a client's disequilibrium. A practitioner may pulse the client and rub his or her body with *aguardiente* to force out a cold, evil wind or some other form of inhabitation after making proper offerings at the family altar. There are three types of inhabitations that are usually extracted.

A feather implies that the curer is removing an evil wind, or *ahmo cualli ehecat,* and that the client must use great care in protecting himself or herself from such winds in the future. The client must not go out alone and must be wary of the night and the forests. In a sense, this forces the client to use his or her social network to avoid being alone in dangerous places.

Animal teeth, claws, and beaks that are extracted suggest witchcraft. One must take great care never to offend a witch, one of his or her close relatives, or anyone suspected of having an *inagual* or animal alter ego that corresponds to the type of animal part extracted. Since practitioners have some fairly clear notions of witchcraft, how it is done, and who in town is capable of doing it, as well as their probable animal alter egos, the object represents in a very real way the practitioner's hypothesis as to the identity of the potential witch. If the client is not sufficiently versed in such arcana, the practitioner will often blatantly tell him or her his suspicions as to the witch's identity.

The third type of object is a clod of dirt, a stone, an obsidian flake, or a pebble. These objects all pertain to the underworld and clearly suggest to a client that he or she has in some way transgressed against the traditions of the holy earth. When such objects are extracted, a practitioner will always prescribe ritual offerings that must be made, some of which can be severely taxing on the client and his or her extended family. Examples include a hen or a turkey, as well as regular offerings throughout the year.

Rituals that seek to manipulate the social system in order to resolve conflict may do so in several ways. The goal, which is not always achieved, is to force individuals to resolve conflicts in everyday life in order to restore a fellow villager's soul to equilibrium. Individuals who refuse to participate in such activities are frowned upon in the village and are often targets of witchcraft by the client's family or even by the practitioner. No one wants a curing to fail, so there is considerable social pressure on everyone to participate.

Making ritual offerings for the supernaturals of the underworld and the sky is the least arduous of ways that a practitioner may attempt to manipulate the social system. A practitioner may simply request that a family leave regular offerings such as food or flowers on their family altars. Or he or she may request a considerably more complex regimen involving many friends and members of the extended family. In a particularly severe situation, the practitioner may request that the family sacrifice many hens or turkeys at a specific site far from the village. Both of the practitioners said that in the past they often requested such offerings at local springs and caves and that they assisted in the necessary rituals, but when I knew them, both were too elderly and infirm for such practices. At that point, they generally requested that several family members and the client go to a site and leave offerings while the practitioner said the proper prayers at his or her home altar. Participants in such offering ceremonies became ritual kin with prescribed patterns of behavior toward each other and the client.

Often, as a part of the ritual prescription for restoring a lost soul, practitioners would ask certain members of the family to participate in pilgrimages for the Virgin of the Remedies, the Virgin of Guadalupe, or Ocotlan. For villagers these were long and arduous journeys, despite the fact that most take the bus now. One of the practitioners mentioned that his father had taken him to several caves and a hot spring, but that these places were no longer places of pilgrimage. Few people other than him knew where they were. Requesting a ritual journey displaces the participants from both the village and its social networks, forcing them to share an experience and a journey and to rely on one another in ways that wouldn't be possible in the village. They are thus forced by the situation to resolve conflicts of everyday life in the village. These people did not become ritual kin but were virtually such by the time they returned.

Practitioners also requested that family members contract ritual kinship obligations in the more standard ways as part of curing—through sponsorship of baptism, communion, and more recently confirmation and marriage. This type of ritual kinship was considered far more permanent than assisting other more common types of ritual kinship. The social and financial obligations were also far more taxing on a family's resources, and this was not a common request.

THE DIALOGUE OF EARTH AND SKY

In order to maintain life on earth, mankind balances between two opposing worlds of the supernatural. The underworld of the ancestors represents the tradition and natural philosophy that link mankind to the holy earth, *talocan*. This is a complex, coherent, and complete system that in and of itself seeks to maintain the balance necessary for life on the earth. It is based on traditional notions of the soul, the form and structure of the underworld, curing, direct experience of the supernatural, interpretation and analysis of dreams, and ritual methods of restoring that fundamental equilibrium when its balance is violated. This system is not a mere remnant of the bygone glory of Aztec cosmovision. It is a functioning system based on fundamental principles of Mesoamerican cosmovision. The system that emerges from the dialogical process of dreaming and curing is an integral part of everyday life in the Sierra de Puebla today.

Tlalocan, the underworld of the Aztecs, was not devoured by the Spanish conquest. The ravenous horde thirsting for gold that consumed the Aztec Empire could not snuff out what people held in their hearts and minds. Political, economic, and religious institutions were destroyed, but try as they might, the rulers and evangelizers of New Spain could not extinguish fundamental Mesoamerican ideology.

The system of beliefs in the Sierra de Puebla today concerning the earth, the ancestors, the soul, and the underworld shares this ancient Mesoamerican cosmovision. It is not a product of syncretism, nor is it in any way a mere vestige of the Aztec Empire. As Barbara Tedlock (1983) pointed out for highland Guatemala, the notion of religion being a "fused," "welded," or "blended" amalgamation of colonial, Hispanic, and native traditions is not productive. Beliefs concerning the underworld of their ancestors, *talocan,* in the Sierra Nahuat dialect of the people of San Martín Zinacapan, represent a clear, coherent cosmovision with firm Mesoamerican roots. It is a natural philosophy based on the dialectical conception of the necessary harmony between the earth, the sky, and the water that is "guaranteed by ritual" today (Broda 1987: 106). It emerges from the dialogue of earth and sky.

SERVING THE MOST HOLY EARTH

Though this may seem an esoteric tradition linked to all kinds of obscure pre-Columbian beliefs, its primary focus is serving people by helping them to deal with life's crises. There is no crisis more profound than an imminent death in the family. As a servant of the Most Holy Earth, it was my obligation to help a dear friend find her way in the underworld of her ancestors.

JANUARY 22, 2000

Lina had called last night. She asked me to pick her up early this morning with young Miguel. As we drove from Puebla to the Sierra, we stopped in a small town in the foothills of La Malinche, the stark volcanic mountain that dominates the northeastern side of the Valley of Puebla.

In the town of San Miguel we picked up Don Pablo, the fourth member of our party. He directed us along a torturous road skirting the volcano to a point where we had to leave the car and walk. After about an hour of walking, Pablo led us to a cave under an outcropping of rock. The floor of the cave was strewn with stones, some the size of apples, others as large as watermelons, and some even larger. Pablo knew exactly the stones we needed. These were the *tetoani,* 'the stones that speak.' They weren't too large, and I could see no distinguishing marks on them that differentiated them from all of the other stones on the cave floor, but Pablo assured us that the five stones he selected were the ones we wanted.

We trekked back down through the forest in a light drizzle, put the stones in the trunk, and headed back to the main road to the Sierra de Puebla. We were on our way up to the Sierra for a ritual I had never participated in before, something called *icxi taltoca,* 'planting the feet in the earth.' I had asked Lina what I had to do last night when she called, but as usual she told me she would explain everything when the time came.

We were on our way up to the Sierra to see the wife of a dear friend. His father had been one of my teachers in San Martín. I had known Dionisio and Carmen since they married when he was seventeen and she was fifteen. People marry young in the Sierra.

Carmen was dying. It was the second recurrence of a cancer that had ravaged her body for the last two years. She had been hospitalized twice in Puebla, but the treatments had not succeeded. She had returned to the Sierra with her husband two weeks earlier.

The Sierra Norte de Puebla is forever lost in the fogs of cloud forests. The town of San Martín is at the end of a long and treacherous winding mountain road that passes through Zacopoaxtla and then Cuetzalan. I came around the last curve into Cuetzalan and drove on past the great stone cathedral of San Francisco with its tower reaching up into the afternoon clouds. The old bell tower that once served as a lookout against the invading French armies and now houses the town clock, stood in the center of the town gardens tolling the lost hours. The gardens were laid out at the end of the last century, vertically perched between the church plaza and the town's market. I kept on driving right through the town in the rain and the fog, to the jeep trail at the end of the road that led to San Martín Zinacapan a few kilometers further into the mountains.

We parked the car near the town square and made our way down to Dionisio's house carrying all of the things we had brought with us. Lina, young Miguel, and Don Pablo set about arranging things on Dionisio's family altar. I went in to see Carmen. She was obviously in pain, but she seemed delighted to see me. All of the medication she was taking for the pain made her sleepy. Her eyes told me that she was weaving in and out of consciousness.

Her daughter Juana came in and then Ramos, her son. We all just sat there not saying much. Finally Dionisio came in and told us it was time to bring Carmen into the main room. The four of us carried her on the bed to a place in front of the family altar. The bed had been borrowed from a neighbor. Most people sleep on mats on the floor in San Martín. The bed was a concession to the fact that Carmen was terminally ill.

It was growing dark. Slowly friends and family began to arrive bearing flowers, candles, incense, packets of cigarettes or hand-rolled cigars made from local tobacco, *aguardiente,* the fiery local alcohol, sweet breads, and tortillas. All these things were placed on the family altar.

Lina took me aside and hastily explained the evening's order of business. She would begin with a prayer to the Most Holy Earth, light the candles and incense, and then each of us would say a short prayer, light a candle, and place offerings on the altar, beginning with Miguel and then Pablo. I would follow Pablo, and Dionisio would say the final prayer. Then Pablo would take 'the stones that speak' from below the altar where he had placed them and explain what we were to do with them.

Things were crowded and more than a bit chaotic with friends and family sitting on borrowed chairs around the edge of the room. People walked in and out as Lina began. Carmen was only half-conscious, but she smiled when her children held her hand. We each said our prayers and made our offerings. Then Don Pablo lifted the stones from under the altar, calling each of them by name and placing them on the altar. He spoke a highland dialect of Nahuatl, but most of the people in the room could understand it. He gave each of us a stone and told us to hold the stone to our hearts. He gave Dionisio the stone he called the heart of *Tlalocan,* the center of the underworld. He told us that we were the pillars of the underworld and that we should each ask the stone we held to speak to our heart.

Don Pablo then asked Lena to begin. She held the stone that was the Heart of the West. She began with a short prayer in Otomi that she said she had learned from her mother. She explained the prayer in Spanish and then began to recount to Carmen all of the things she would see in the west, the house of women and the mountain of the sun, the life women led in the house of women. When she finished, Miguel began, also with a prayer he had learned from his mother. He explained the cave of the winds in the north of the underworld. Don Pablo then prayed and talked of the abundance of the great sea of the east. I began with a short prayer I had learned from Rubia asking for the holy light of the sky to help me speak of the world of darkness, and then I explained the south of the underworld to Carmen.

Dionisio began with a prayer his father had used. He then named both his and his wife's ancestors who had entered into the underworld. He asked them to help Carmen find her way in the world of darkness. He described the center of *talocan*. He asked the lords and ladies of the underworld to help his wife find her way in the darkness. At this point he was weeping, as were most of us. He finished with a request that the true lord of darkness, the *taloc melauh,* welcome his wife, and he placed the stone on her heart. Carmen asked that she be welcomed by her ancestors.

Then Dionisio asked his daughter to bring out some refreshments for everyone, and he began to distribute the sweet bread from the altar. Don Pablo took the *aguardiente* from the altar and began to offer small glasses to everyone as well. We stayed until nearly dawn and returned to Puebla the next day. Doña Carmen joined her ancestors less than a week later.

NOTES

Chapter 1

1. The dialect spoken in this region leads directly to the notion of Toltec ancestry (see Knab 1983b).

2. For a discussion of the shaman-priest problem, see B. Tedlock 1982: 46–84.

3. Throughout this book, I use a modified version of Tedlock's (1971) method of transcribing style in oral narrative with line breaks for breath pauses and extra spaces for shorter pauses. These texts are meant to be read aloud.

4. Karttunen (1983) notes the anomalous nature of the derivation of the name of Tlaloc.

5. As the generalized bound form, I am using *i-*, 'his or hers,' *mo-*, 'your,' and *no-*, 'my,' rather than the indefinite *te-*, 'someone's' (which is almost never heard in everyday speech in Sierra Nahuat) to distinguish bound from unbound forms.

6. Signorini and Lupo (1989) are essentially correct on semantic grounds in considering the *ecahuil* as an alternate part of the soul. 'Shadow' or *ecahuil* is the common term used in referring to the dark cold aspects of the soul shared with the *nagual*.

7. See my discussion of the *tonal* as well as figures 2 and 3, which when rotated are almost the exact equivalent of Signorini and Lupo's (1989: 77) representation with different labels.

8. A watery heart is one that longs for the waters of the East. This region of the underworld is a paradise of abundance and water from which souls are loath to depart. Thus the heart is slothful and lazy.

9. In ribald puns, the new ear of corn is the erect penis from which the seeds of next year's crop come forth. The leaves are its hands or arms, and the tassel the head and hair.

10. Inocente learned quite a bit about this while he worked as a hired gun for a local *cacique* (see Knab 1995).

Chapter 2

1. It's a fairly common practice in the Sierra to tie a strip of cloth around an infant's head to keep the soul in.

2. Martín's wife and Ramos' mother.

3. A monumental effort to preserve traditions is being made by the *Taller de Tradición Oral of the Sociedad agropecuaria del CEPEC, S. de S.S.*, which has thus far published thirteen short volumes of local oral traditions. The *taller* has also published a collection of tales with the INAH that is nearly 600 pages long called *Tejuan Tikintenkakiliayaj in toueyitajuan: Les oímos contar a nuestros abuelos: Etnohistoria de San Miguel Tzinacapan.*

4. I am using the term 'dreamtale' to distinguish between a trained practitioner's way of using the dream narrative in the context of curing a client and the dream narratives told in casual conversation in the village. This is not a standard genre distinction in Nahuat.

5. A tape recorder. The word is borrowed from Spanish.

6. There is only one account of an individual wounded in battle, either in the French invasion or in the early stages of the Mexican Revolution, who became a practitioner. This individual was the ancestor of one of the curers with whom I worked.

7. These are varieties of masked dancers common in the region.

8. This is a large area of flat rocks below San Andres where many women go to do their wash. It is an area that Chela and her family would know well as it is near their cornfields.

9. On special occasions, Sanmartinos still wear large headdresses made of purple and green strands of wool wound together with the hair of ancestors. Donald and Dorothy Cordry (1940: 51–55 and 1968: 225–30) describe this type of headgear but don't mention the strands of hair of the ancestors. In a way, a woman carries the tradition of all her female ancestors woven into her headdress.

Rubia also noted that the women were wearing the light, white, cotton skirts of summer rather than their winter ones of heavy, dark wool. She was possibly indicating that this was a warm place in the underworld.

Chapter 3

1. Prayers are not raised up in San Martín. They are lowered, *temoa*. They are humbly mumbled in the cave, before the family altars, or even before the altar of the church of San Martín.

2. The orthography used here is a modification of Classical Nahuatl orthography adapted to Sierra Nahuat. Phonological, morphological, and syntactic modifications of everyday Nahuat form that are characteristic of prayer have been preserved in these texts, which may make them seem unusual to those familiar with Nahuatl. For example, in the first line, *-maca*, give, is written *maga* as the velar consonant is voiced in the mumbled prayer. What would be standard word division as in *xinechmaga*, give him to me, is also modified to fit with the cadence or meter of the prayer, which is pronounced as three segments with three primary accents: *áxcan xínech mága*. The metric is an essential part of prayer that gives it an almost hypnotic, litany-like quality. In general, lines correspond to what Robinson (1969:21) termed 'mesosegments.' Often, these segments are run together in prayer, yet they can be distinguished on the basis of scansion and structural parallelisms. Final intonational contours are indicated with standard punctuation, which takes into account morphological considerations as well, indicating interrogatives and imperatives. Pauses longer than normal word pauses are indicated with extra spaces within lines.

3. Here the reference has changed; this is indicated with a space between lines.

4. This is discussed far more adequately in the paper "*Geografía del inframundo*" (Knab 1991) and in chapter 4.

5. There is a switch in reference here, which is indicated by a space between lines as well as a long pause indicated by a double slash.

6. This is far more clear than in Aramoni's (1990: 161–76) treatment of the dualism inherent in such concepts.

7. There continues here a long litany of places that are found in the underworld.

8. This prayer is said after the sun has set. It must be ended quickly for night is a dangerous time. It is the time of *talocan,* and the supernaturals of the sky might not hear this plea.

Chapter 4

1. Limestone formations in the Sierra de Puebla often have the appearance of tree bark.

2. The edges of the natural world and the sky are defined by the same features that define the four sides of the underworld.

3. See further on in chapter 4 for a discussion of the role of numbers in naming the indeterminate locations in the underworld.

4. Fulano indicates anyone, similar to the term John Doe.

5. For the people of the Sierra de Puebla, north is considered to be the entire northern region, from the northeast to the northwest. The actual directions in this case are lines that divide the directions. The intercardinal directions NE and NW define the North, SE and SW define the South, NE and SE define the East. See Folio 1 in Codex Féjévary-Mayer 1971, for example. Here it is also worthwhile to note that the most common metaphor for the underworld is the flower with four petals, which serves as a common schematic of *talocan* as an axis with four sides (Knab 1991) and that this flower is the same as Teotihuacán's ubiquitous decorative motif (Heyden 1985).

6. See Thelma D. Sullivan's (1982) work on Tlazoteotl for a description of the *temascal* as an entry to the underworld.

7. The plaza of the great temple of Tenochtitlan (Matos Moctezuma 1987) was not only an axis of the world but a model for it that was based on the same natural philosophy (Broda 1987).

8. This may not be a reference to the historic Chichimecs; the term has become a general derogative. This particular practitioner was quite literate, and when I first asked him about prayers and ancient stories, he read me several sections from Father Garibay's *Llave del Náhuatl* (1956).

9. According to numerous tales, the assistants are toads who keep the pots (Knab 1983a).

10. This 'church' of the underworld is strikingly similar to the cave found at the base of the Pyramid of the Sun in Teotihuacán (Heyden, 1975; 1981), which may have served the same purpose for the priests of Teotihuacán as the cave that is the 'church' of the underworld served. Though Heyden points out the cave's similarity to the *Chicomostoc,* the seven caves of origin of the Aztec peoples, and the cave of Teotihuacán, it may have also served as the primordial sanctuary of the underworld. An entire network of caves has recently been discovered under Teotihuacán, left over from mining activities (Manzanilla et al. 1989 and Barba et al. 1990). It may also have served this function. It is not unusual in Mesoamerica for sacred spaces to exhibit a variety of symbolism. In fact, the more meaning packed into a space, the more potent it was.

11. Toads in the Sierra do not actually have prominent teeth. There are many biting insects on the floors of the region's many caves, and a short walk inside will leave one's ankles bleeding. Because toads are one of the few species one can see on cave floors, the bites are often mistakenly attributed to them, and many people assume that they have long, sharp teeth. Perhaps the teeth of the toad and the nocturnal eyes combined to form the basis for images of *Tlaloc* in ancient Mesoamerica.

12. As explained earlier, it is very dangerous to reveal your *nonagual*. In the process of training, Rubia had already told me about her primary *nonagual* as well as many others that she had learned to take on for her journeys in the underworld.

13. The *tepeyolomeh* can be both the enchanted places in the underworld and the animate embodiment of such places. They are classified with the *talocanca*.

14. The women of San Martín intertwine the hairs of their ancestors into their headdresses, but the *miquicihuauh*, death woman, has hairs of all the ancestors in her headdress.

15. Today in the Sierra de Puebla, *ocuillin* is the more common term for 'animal.' *Yolcat* is an archaism that implies a ferocious or evil animal.

16. Kirchoff implicitly recognized the conceptual unity of Mesoamerica in his original paper as well as in his later work on ideology and superstructure of the deities and their festivals. Toward the end of his life, he would readily explain to friends and students that his long lists and tables of traits were in fact shorthand for a conceptual system that unified human thought and linked people across cultural boundaries through social processes.

Chapter 5

1. These are the traditional wrapped skirts that are worn by the women in the Sierra today.

2. Both practitioners began to explain how *naguals* are acquired.

3. This is also a metaphor in Nahuat, as it is for us, for leading a good life, *cualli nehnemi*.

4. This is a metaphor for having sexual intercourse as it is in many areas of Mesoamerica (Tarn and Prechtel, 1990).

5. The orchards are a favorite place for illicit sexual activity (Knab 1983a: 281–304).

6. These fruits do not ripen at the same time, indicating that this is a mystical setting.

7. They are considered sexually hyperactive and bisexual.

BIBLIOGRAPHY

Aguirre Beltran, Gonzalo
1983 La sombra y el animal: La medicina tradicional, in *La medicina invisible*, X. Lozoya and C. Zolla, eds., Folios Ediciones: Mexico City, pp. 104–29.

Almeida, Eduardo
1987 Don Inocensio Flores de La Cruz de San Miguel Tzinacapan Puebla, in *Los chamanes de México: Psicología autóctona mexicana* (vol. 1), Jacobo Grinberg-Zylberbaum, ed., Alpa Corral: Mexico City, pp. 111–28.

Aramoni, María Elena
1990 *Talokan Tata, Talokan Nana: Nuestras raíces; Hierofanías y testimonios de un mundo indígena,* Consejo Nacional para la Cultura y las Artes: Mexico City.

Attinasi, John, and Paul Friedrich
1995 Dialogic Breakthrough: Catalysis and Synthesis in Life-Changing Dialogue, in *The Dialogic Emergence of Culture,* Dennis Tedlock and Bruce Mannheim, eds., University of Illinois Press: Urbana, IL, pp. 33–53.

Aveni, A. F., E. E. Calnek, and H. Hartung
1988 Myth, Environment, and the Orientation of the Templo Mayor of Tenochtitlan, *American Antiquity* 53(2), pp. 287–309.

Bachelard, Gaston
1969 *The Poetics of Reverie,* Daniel Russel, trans., Beacon Press: Boston, MA.

Bakhtin, Mikhail
1968 *Rabelais and His World,* H. Iswolsky, trans., MIT Press: Cambridge, MA.
1981 *The Dialogic Imagination: Four Essays by M. M. Bakhtin,* M. Holquist, ed., C. Emerson and M. Holquist, trans., University of Texas Press: Austin, TX.
1986 *Speech Genres and other Late Essays,* C. Emerson and M Holquist, eds., V. McGee, trans., University of Texas Press: Austin, TX.

Barba, Luis A., Linda Manzanilla, R. Chávez, Luis Flores, and A. J. Azate
1990   Caves and Tunnels at Teotihuacán, Mexico; A Geological Phenomena of Archaeological Interest, in *Archaeological Geology of North America,* N. P. Lacsa and J. Donahue, eds., Geological Society of America, Centennial Special Volume 4, Boulder, CO.

Bateson, Gregory
1974   *Steps to an Ecology of Mind,* Chandler: San Francisco, CA.

Bateson, Gregory, and Mary Catherine Bateson
1988   *Angel's Fear: Towards an Epistemology of the Sacred,* Bantam Books: New York, NY.

Boege, Eckart
1988   *Los mazatecos ante la nación: Contradicciones de la identidad étnica en el México actual,* Siglo Veintiuno: Mexico City.

Bonfil, Guillermo
1990   *México profundo,* Grijalbo: Mexico City.

Bourdieu, Pierre
1977   *Outline of a Theory of Practice,* R. Nice, trans., Cambridge University Press: Cambridge.

Brinton, Daniel G.
1894   Nagualism, A Study of Native American Folklore and History, in *Proceedings of the American Philosophical Society,* XXXIII, 144: pp. 11–73.

Broda, Johanna
1987   The Templo Mayor as Ritual Space, in *The Great Temple of Tenochtitlan: Center and Periphery in the Aztec World,* J. Broda, D. Carrasco, and E. Matos Moctezuma, eds., University of California Press: Berkeley, CA, pp. 61–123.
1991 The Sacred Landscape of the Aztec Calendar Festivals: Myth, Nature, and Society, in To Change Place: Aztec Ceremonial Landscapes, D. Carrasco, ed., University Press of Colorado: Niwot, CO, pp. 74–120.

Bruce, Robert D.
1975   *Lacandon Dream Symbolism,* 2 vols., Ediciones Euroamericanas: Mexico City.

Carrasco, Davíd

1990   *Religions of Mesoamerica: Cosmovision and Ceremonial Centers,* Harper San Francisco: San Francisco, CA.

Clark, Katerina, and Michael Holquist

1984   *Mikhail Bakhtin,* Belknap Press, Harvard University: Cambridge, MA.

Codex, Féjévary-Mayer

1971   Akademische Druck- und Verlagsanstalt: Graz, Austria.

Cordry, Donald B. and Dorothy M. Cordry

1940 Costumes and textiles of the Aztec Indians of the Cuetzalan region Puebla Mexico, in *Southwest Museum Papers,* No. 14, Southwest Museum: Highland Park, Los Angeles, CA.

1968 *Mexican Indian Costumes,* University of Texas Press: Austin, TX.

Foster, George M.

1944   Nagualism in Mexico and Guatemala, in *Actas Americanas,* II, no. 1 & 2: pp. 85–103.

Garibay, Angel María

1956   *Llave del Náhuatl,* Porrua: Mexico City.

Gonzalez Torres, Yolotl

1976   El Concepto de Tona en el México Antiguo, in *Boletín del Instituto Nacional de Antropología e Historia,* 19 (2), pp. 13–16.

Gossen, Gary

1974   *Chamulas in the World of the Sun: Time and Space in Maya Oral Tradition,* Harvard University Press: Cambridge, MA.

Grinberg-Zylberbaum, Jacobo, ed.

1987   *Los Chamanes de Mexico,* 6 vols., Alpa Corral: Mexico City.

Gruzinski, Serge

1989   *Man Gods in the Mexican Highlands: Indian Power and Colonial Society 1500–1820,* Eileen Corrigan, trans., Stanford University Press: Palo Alto, CA.

Herdt, Gilbert

1987   Selfhood and Discourse in Sambia Dream Sharing, in *Dreaming: Anthropological and Psychological Interpretations,* B. Tedlock, ed., School for American Research, Cambridge University Press: Cambridge, MA, pp. 55–85.

Heyden, Doris

1975   An Interpretetion of the Cave Underneath the Pyramid of the Sun in Teotihuacán, Mexico, in *American Antiquity,* 40(2), pp. 131–47.

1981   Caves, Gods, and Myths, in *Mesoamerican Sites and World Views,* E. P. Benson, ed., Dumbarton Oaks: Washington, D.C., pp. 1–39.

1985   *Mitologia y Simbolismo de la Flora en el México Prehispánico,* 2nd ed., Universidad Nacional Autónoma de México: Mexico City.

Islas, Elena, and Ma. Eugenia Sánchez

1987   Doña Rufina de Puebla, in *Los Chamanes de Mexico: Misticismo Indigena* (vol. 2), Jacobo Grinberg-Zylberbaum, ed., Alpa Corral: Mexico City, pp. 181–97.

Jung, Carl

1916   The Trancendent Function, in *The Collected Works of C. G. Jung,* vol. 8, R. F. C. Hull, trans., Bollingen Series 20 (1959), Princeton University Press: Princeton, NJ.

Karttunen, F.

1983   *An Analytical Dictionary of Nahuatl,* University of Texas Press: Austin, TX.

Kirchhoff, Paul

1952   Mesoamerica: Its Geographic Limits, Ethnic Composition, and Cultural Characteristics, in *The Heritage of Conquest,* Sol Tax, ed., University of Chicago Press: Chicago, IL.

Knab, Timothy J.

1978   Talocan Talmanic: Supernatural Beings in the Sierra de Puebla, in *Religión y Sociedad, Actes du XLII Congres Internacional des Americanistes,* VI, pp. 127–36.

1980   Three Tales from the Sierra de Puebla, in *Alcheringa,* vol. 4, no. 2, pp. 2–37.

1983a *Words Great and Small: Sierra Nahuat Narrative Discourse in Everyday Life,* Ph.D. dissertation, State University of New York, Albany.

1983b En que hablaban los tepalcates Teotihuacanos? (No era Náhuatl.), *Revista de la Sociedad Mexicana de Antropología,* vol. 29, pp. 145–58.

1984   Metaphors, Concepts, and Coherence in Aztec, in *Symbol and Meaning beyond the Closed Community: Essays in Mesoamerican Ideas,* G. Gossen, ed., IMS/SUNY: Albany, NY, pp. 42–56.

1991   Geografía del inframundo, *Estudios de Cultura Náhuatl,* 21, pp. 31-58.

1995   *A War of Witches: A Journey into the Underworld of the Contemporary Aztecs,* Harper San Francisco: San Francisco, CA.

Laughlin, Robert M.

1976   *Of Wonders Wild and New: Dreams from Zinacantán,* Smithsonian Contributions to Anthropology, no. 22, Smithsonian Institution Press: Washington, D.C.

Léon-Portilla, Miguel

1963   *Aztec Thought and Culture: A Study of the Ancient Nahuatl Mind,* J. E. Davis, trans., University of Oklahoma Press: Norman, OK.

1969   *Pre-Columbian Literatures of Mexico,* University of Oklahoma Press: Norman, OK.

López Austin, Alfredo

1980   *Cuerpo humano e ideología: Las concepciones de los antiguos Nahuas,* 2 vols., Universidad Nacional Autónoma de México, Instituto de Investigaciones Antropológicas: Mexico City.

1994   *Tlalocan y Tamoanchan,* Fondo de Cultura Económica: Mexico City.

Lupo, Alessandro

1995   *La tierra nos escucha: La cosmología de los Nahuas a través de las súplicas rituales,* Stella Mastrangelo, trans., Consejo Nacional para la Cultura y las Artes/Instituto Nacional Indigenista: Mexico City.

McKeever Furst, Jill Leslie

1995   *The Natural History of the Soul in Ancient Mexico,* Yale University Press: New Haven, CT.

Mannheim, Bruce, and Dennis Tedlock

1995   Introduction, in *The Dialogic Emergence of Culture,* Dennis Tedlock and Bruce Mannheim, eds., University of Illinois Press: Urbana, IL, pp. 1–32.

Manzanilla, Linda, Luis Barba, René Chávez, Jorge Arzate, y Leticia Flores

1989   El inframundo de Teotihuácan. Geofísica y arqueología, in *Ciencia y desarollo,* vol. XV, 85, pp. 21–36.

Matos Moctezuma, Eduardo

1987   The Templo Mayor of Tenochtitlan: History and Interpretation, in *The Great Temple of Tenochtitlan: Center and Periphery in the Aztec World,* J. Broda, D. Carrasco, and E. Matos Moctezuma, eds., University of California Press: Berkeley, CA, pp. 15–60.

Motolinía, Fray Torbio de Benavente
1971   *Memoriales o Libro de las Cosas de la Nueva España y de los Naturaled de Ella,* Edmundo O'Gorman, ed., Universidad Nacional Autónoma de México: Mexico City.

Ortiz de Montellano, Bernardo
1990   *Aztec Medicine, Health, and Nutrition,* Rutgers University Press: New Brunswick, NJ.

Price-Williams, Douglas
1987   The Waking Dream in Ethnographic Perspective, in *Dreaming: Anthropological and Psychological Interpretations,* B. Tedlock, ed., School for American Research, Cambridge University Press: Cambridge, pp. 246–262.

Radin, Paul
1955   *Primitive Man as Philosopher,* Dover: New York, NY.

Reyes, Luís
1976   Introducción, in *Der Ring Aus Tlalocan/El Anillo de Tlalocan,* Ibero-Amerikanisches Institut, Quellenwerke zur alten Geschicte Amerikas, Aufgezeichnet in den Sprachen der Eingeborenen 12, Gebr. Mann Verlag: Berlin, pp. 123–35.

Ricoeur, Paul
1970   *Freud and Philosophy: An Essay on Interpretation,* Dennis Savage, trans., Yale University Press: New Haven, CT.
1976   *Interpretation Theory: Discourse and the Surplus of Meaning,* The Texas Christian University Press: Fort Worth, TX.

Robinson, Dow
1969   *Aztec Studies I,* SIL: Mexico City.

Ross, Patricia
1950   Los Mejicanos de Cuetzalan, in *Mesoamerican Notes,* 2, pp. 94–101.

Ruíz de Alarcón, Hernando
1987   *Treaties on the Heathen Superstitions that Today Live among the Indians Native to New Spain, 1629, by Hernando Ruíz de Alarcón,* J. R. Andrews and R. Hassig, trans., University of Oklahoma Press: Norman, OK.

Sandstrom, Alan
1991   *Corn Is Our Blood: Culture and Ethnicity in a Contemporary Aztec Village,* University of Oklahoma Press: Norman, OK.

Schutz, A.
1967 *Phenomenology of the Social World,* Walsh and Lambert, trans., Northwestern University Press: Evanston, IL.

Seler, E.
1963 *Comentarios al Códice Borgia,* Fondo de Cultura Económica: Mexico City.

Signorini, Italo, and Alessandro Lupo
1989 *Los Tres Ejes de la Vida: Almas, cuerpo, enfermidad entre los Nahuas de la Sierra de Puebla,* Editorial de la Universidad Veracruzana Xalapa: Veracruz, MX.

Sullivan, Thelma D.
1965 A Prayer to Tlaloc, in *Estudios de la cultura Náhuatl,* vol. 5, pp. 39–55.
1972 Tlaloc: A New Etymological Interpretation of the God's Name and What It Reveals of His Essence and Nature, in *Acti del XL Congreso Internacionale Degli Americanisti,* II, pp. 213–19.
1982 *Tlazoteotl Ixcuina:* The Great Spinner and Weaver, in *The Art and Iconography of the Later Post-Classic Central Mexico,* E. H. Boone, ed., Dumbarton Oaks Research Center: Washington, D.C., pp. 7–35.

Taggart, James M.
1983 *Nahuat Myth and Social Structure,* University of Texas Press: Austin, TX.

Taller de Tradición Oral of the Sociedad agropecuaria del CEPEC
1978–1990, *Traditiones orales de nuestros abuelos,* 14 vols., CEPEC: San Miguel Tzinacapan, Puebla.
1994 *Tejuan Tikintenkakiliayaj in toueyitajuan: Les oímos contar a nuestros abuelos: Etnohistoria de San Miguel Tzinacapan,* INAH: México City.

Tarn, Nathaniel, and Martín Prechtel
1990 'Comiéndose la fruta': Metáforas sexuales e iniciaciones en Santiago Atitlán, in *Mesoamérica,* 19, pp. 73–82.

Tedlock, Barbara
1982 *Time and the Highland Maya,* University of New Mexico Press: Albuquerque, NM (revised ed., 1992).
1983 A Phenomenological Approach to Religious Change in Highland Guatemala, in *The Heritage of Conquest Thirty Years Later,* Carl Kendall, John Hawkins, and Laurel Bossen, eds., University of New Mexico Press: Albuquerque, NM, pp. 235–46.

Tedlock, Barbara, ed.
1987   *Dreaming: Anthropological and Psychological Interpretations,* School for American Research, Cambridge University Press: Cambridge.

Tedlock, Dennis
1971 On the Translation of Style in Oral Narrative, in *Journal of American Folklore,* 84, pp. 114–33.
1983   *The Spoken Word and the Work of Interpretation,* University of Pennsylvania Press: Philadelphia, PA.
1995 Interpretation, Participation, and the Role of Narrative in Dialogical Anthropology, in *The Dialogic Emergence of Culture,* Dennis Tedlock and Bruce Mannheim, eds., University of Illinois Press: Urbana, IL, pp. 253–87.

Tedlock, Dennis, and Bruce Mannheim, eds.
1995   *The Dialogic Emergence of Culture,* University of Illinois Press: Urbana, IL.

Tedlock, Dennis, and Barbara Tedlock
1985 Text and Textile: Language and Technology in the Arts of the Quiche Maya, in *Journal of Anthropological Research,* 41(20), pp. 121–46.

Todorov, Tzvetan
1982a *La Conquête de l'Amérique: La question de l'autre,* Éditions du Seuil: Paris.
1982b *Symbolism and Interpretation,* C. Porter, trans., Cornell University Press: Ithaca, NY.
1984   *Mikhail Bakhtin: The Dialogical Principle,* Wlad Godzich, trans., University of Minnesota Press: Minneapolis, MN.

Torquemada, Fray Juan de
1943   *Monarquía Indiana. Los Veintiun Libros Rituales,* facsimile of the 1723 edition, 3 vol., Editorial Chavez Hayhoe: Mexico City.

Turner, Victor
1974   *Dramas, Fields, and Metaphors,* Cornell University Press: Ithaca, NY.

Villa Rojas, Alfonso
1963 El Nagualismo como recurso de control social entre grupos mayences de Chiapas, México, *Estudios de cultura Maya,* III, pp. 243–60.

Voloshinov, V. N./M. M. Bakhtin
1973 *Marxism and the Philosophy of Language,* Ladislav Matejka and I. R. Titunik, trans., Seminar Press: New York, NY.

Wicke, C., and F. Horcasitas
1957 Archaeological Investigations on Mount Tlaloc, Mexico, in *Mesoamerican Notes,* 5, pp. 83–97.

Wisdom, Charles
1940 *The Chorti Indians of Guatemala,* University of Chicago Press: Chicago, IL.

Wolf, Eric
1987 *Sons of the Shaking Earth,* University of Chicago Press: Chicago, IL.

INDEX

concept of, 24–28
cosmic location of, 26, 27
loss of, 32–33, 38, 151
naming of, 14, 24
nature of, 31–33
possessive form of, 29–30
wanderings of, 33, 42
tonalism, 36
tonallan, 112–113
trees, 99, 116

underworld. *See* talocan

War of the Witches, 36, 56, 70

water, 110–111
witch (*nagualli*), 24, 32, 34, 35–37
witchcraft, 31, 35–37, 151, 153

xochicuauhuit, 99

yolcatagat, 126
-*yollo* (*no-*, *mo-*, *i-*), 11
concept of, 24–28
cosmic location of, 26, 27
damage to, 38, 151
naming of, 14
nature of, 30–31
possessive form of, 29–30

ABOUT THE AUTHOR

AN ANTHROPOLOGIST AND LINGUIST by profession as well as a classically trained educator, administrator, and chef, Timothy J. Knab has taught anthropology, religion, English, and linguistics at institutions such as Tufts University, Wellesley College, and the French Culinary Institute in New York. He now teaches at the Universidad de las Américas, Puebla in Cholula. Dr. Knab has also worked in many countries as a consultant, project administrator, and researcher for such organizations as the American Philosophical Society, the National Geographic Society, the National University of Mexico, and the Organization of American States. He has written numerous articles for international publications, and has written and edited four books, including *A Scattering of Jades: Stories, Poems, and Prayers of the Aztecs* (University of Arizona Press, 2003), *A War of Witches: A Journey into the Underworld of the Contemporary Aztecs* (1995) and *Mad Jesus: The Final Testament of a Huichol Messiah from Northwest Mexico* (2004). He has organized conferences and publications for various groups in a wide range of disciplines, and in addition to his academic work, Dr. Knab has earned accolades for his proficiency as a chef, sommelier, writer, and photographer. He is also an avid trekker, skier, outdoorsman, and conservationist.

CPSIA information can be obtained at www.ICGtesting.com
Printed in the USA
LVOW090222101111

254328LV00001B/7/P